IN SEARCH OF BIRDS

Their Haunts & Habitats

JIM FLEGG

ILLUSTRATED BY
NORMAN ARLOTT

BLANDFORD PRESS
POOLE · DORSET

First published in the U.K. 1983
by Blandford Press, Link House,
West Street, Poole, Dorset, BH15 1LL.

Copyright © 1983 Blandford Books Ltd.

Distributed in the United States by
Sterling Publishing Co., Inc.,
2 Park Avenue, New York, N.Y. 10016.

British Library Cataloguing in Publication Data

Flegg, Jim
  In search of birds.
  1. Bird watching
  I. Title
  598'.07'234   QL677.5

ISBN 0 7137 1223 6

Typeset by Megaron Typesetting, Bournemouth.

Printed in Great Britain by Trade Litho Book Printers, Bodmin, Cornwall.

Contents

To my young sons, Matthew and William,
I would like to dedicate this book,
in the hope that, over the course of time,
they too will derive as much enjoyment as I have
from the countryside and its birds.

Preface

For over thirty years, birds and birdwatching have fascinated me. What began as a schoolboy pastime developed into a hobby with a considerable commitment in time and energy, and eventually led to a professional involvement with birds. As a research worker, my concern, naturally enough, has been with understanding the underlying bird biology, but more particularly with bird (and bird habitat) conservation, with the many facets of birds' interactions with mankind, and in particular with birds as pests of crops. Thanks in no small measure to my job, but also because of a deep personal interest, there has been a great deal of travel in my life, both within Britain and Ireland and overseas — hence *In Search of Birds*.

Over and above the largely aesthetic pleasure of just *looking* at birds (contrary to popular belief, research workers do indulge in such delights) are to be found the enjoyments of *watching* birds and attempting to understand more about their lives, their movements and their ecology. In addition, of course, birdwatching can be practised anytime and anywhere, and because even common birds are so versatile that they retain their charm and interest there is no ceiling to their fascination, no matter how skilful or experienced you may become.

This is not a book of where-to-go and what-to-see in a gazetteer or guide-book format, but an introductory explanation of what you are likely to see, when and why it is there — wherever you may be. This is a broad area of birdwatching that seems to me to be relatively poorly represented in the many books available (*see* the Further Reading list) when so many aspects are covered so well. The layout is based on a simple habitat classification:

estuaries, wetlands, farmland, woodland, uplands and the coast, with additional chapters on less usual birds and the bird observatories, European birdwatching and the world scene.

To save packing the text with masses of basic detail on bird identification, a 'beginner's knowledge' of our birds is assumed: the choice of excellent field guides to help in this direction is wide, so this should present no problem. Equally, although there are hints and cautions on how to get the best out of birdwatching in the various habitats, I have taken it for granted that the one essential, binoculars (magnification ×8 to ×10), will be available, and that clothing and footwear suitable both to the habitat and the climate will be worn; there seems to be little point in creating difficulty or discomfort.

Differences in bird distribution in a geographical sense, or in choice of habitat, have been outlined using as examples more detailed accounts of selected species' life histories. In this way I hope that not only may the birds of any area be better understood and enjoyed, but that birdwatching further afield, or in greater depth, may be successfully planned. Although concentrating on Britain and Ireland, the potential benefits, and thrills, of travelling overseas are outlined.

At Blandford Press, Beth Young and Alison Copland have been of great help during the production of this book. Norman Arlott has produced the line drawings, which are not only elegant and extremely attractive in themselves but accurately reflect the anatomy and behaviour of the birds they portray — no mean feat. In addition, they open a pictorial window, throwing a new light on my views on those birds and my feelings for them, and this helps and greatly enlivens the paragraphs of text. Caroline, my wife, has also made a major contribution to the book. Not only has she typed the manuscript, dealing with countless marginal additions and deletions, tidying the grammar, punctuation and spelling as she went, but I have had the benefits of her support and fruitful advice throughout.

Jim Flegg
1983

1 Estuary Saga

Estuaries are sheltered shallow inlets, often with a layout as complex as a river delta, where sea meets river at the turn of the tide. Shallow seas are warm and rich in food in the form of mineral and organic nutrients, and this richness is enhanced by the additional nutrient materials carried down, along with the silt, in the land water draining into the river. Thus an estuary, no matter whether it is sandy or muddy, or in between, contains copious plant life, and each square metre of mudflat usually contains literally millions of small animals, from worms, shellfish and crustaceans to the myriad nematodes and the like among the microscopic invertebrate animals. All of this forms part of food chains supporting larger animals like fish and (perhaps especially in the case of estuaries) birds, often in tremendous numbers.

Then there is the aesthetic angle. Often lonely, few places can be so severe as an estuary, a flat landscape covered by an apparently limitless bowl of ever-changing sky. The mind's eye conjures up a picture of such wild places, the terrestrial evidence of man vanishing as the sea approaches, with a skein of geese in an open V formation against the sunset, with a burning line of sun running across the creek-interrupted mudflats. The mind's ear adds the distant laughing cackle of the geese, with (nearer at hand) some wader calls: the musical lilt of the Curlew or the plaintive whistle of a Grey Plover.

The mudflats themselves, and the saltings islands laced with minute runnels, have much the same appearance year round. The saltings seem grey even in summer; the leaves of the tough grasses and the ever-present oval-leaved sea purslane see to that. In summer, this grey carpet is given some

1

coloured pattern as plants flower: sea asters (like miniature michaelmas daisies), sea lavender (like a spray of blue 'everlasting flowers'), golden-flowered samphire, and glasswort (thick and fleshy, with the appearance of an overweight Christmas tree only a few inches high).

The vegetation has to be tolerant of a wide range of salinities coupled with regular drying-out and inundation as the tides ebb and flow. On the mudflats themselves, an alga called sea lettuce abounds, looking as limp as the worst a motorway café could present; and an odd plant called *Zostera*, or eel grass, which like the sea lettuce is beloved by Brent Geese and Wigeon, helps spread a green sheen. Sea lettuce, and the conspicuous clumps of *Spartina*, looking like its name 'rice-grass', harbour millions of tiny snails, and these the Shelduck relish as noisily as an Italian slurping up his spaghetti.

Spartina clumps tend to collect silt between the bases of the stems, and over the years may accumulate enough to raise the soil level sufficiently for other plants to gain a roothold. Glasswort is one of the first of these, with notorious autumnal colours, and in time a new island may form to replace those lost elsewhere in the estuary to wave erosion.

The tremendous range of available food is reflected in the variety of feeding adaptations, especially among the wading birds. There are the short-billed feeders on the rocks at the foot of the sea wall. Here there is usually a good growth of various bladder-wrack seaweeds, sombre browns, olives and yellows, and against this background the Turnstone is magnificently camouflaged, as is the Rock Pipit, one of the very small song birds to frequent such places. On sandy or pebble beaches, usually some distance above the high water mark, the sandy-coloured Ringed Plover darts about, picking up small insects and other animals. Though the adult is well camouflaged, Ringed Plover eggs and chicks, looking exactly like sand flecked with fragments of shell and dried seaweed, are so well concealed as to be at risk from an unwary human foot.

On the mud or sand flats a number of short-billed waders probe for small animals just beneath the surface. Smallest of these is the Sanderling, usually found (as its name implies) on sandy substrates and easily recognised by its white and silver-grey plumage. Even more characteristic is its run across the sand, when the legs move so quickly that they become just a blur. At the top end of the size scale is the Grey Plover, silver-grey but with copious black flecks, with a white belly in winter that turns jet-black in spring and summer. In flight, the Grey Plover shows strikingly black armpits. Grey Plovers are relatively solitary birds when feeding, and are often to be seen dotted about amongst the masses of other birds, conspicuous because of their hunch-backed bulk.

In most estuaries, the two most numerous species are Dunlin and Knot, both of which fall in the medium length beak size range. The smaller waders, like Dunlin, seem to arrive mysteriously on the mudflats, materialising from twisting shimmering flocks looking almost like smoke in the distance. So precise is the timing of their aerial acrobatics that a dense-packed flock, with birds only inches apart, will turn as one, giving a sudden change from white undersides to grey-brown backs. How this timing is achieved, and why collisions in mid-air are so few, is not properly understood, beyond the fact that birds' eyesight and reflexes seem far superior to man's. Dunlins are amongst the first waders to scamper about on freshly exposed mud as the tide recedes, leaving little lines of beak probe holes between their footprints as they feed. Similar in colouration but larger in size is the Knot. Knot tend to feed in close-packed flocks, but they pack in so close together on their roosts that it is easy to see how they acquired their name.

Also in the medium-billed size range, but larger-bodied, fits the Oystercatcher, often called sea-pie because of its black-and-white plumage.

Oystercatchers

Some Oystercatchers probe for worms both in the estuary mud and on the damp fields in northern Britain where they spend the summer and breed. Others, fascinatingly, specialise in shellfish. Some become adept at creeping silently up to limpets and dislodging them with a sharp tap of the beak, whereas others are expert at prising open mussel shells. Their strong beak is chisel-ended, and flattened from side to side, so that the tip can be inserted in the merest crack to force the shell open; then a scissor-like action quickly severs the muscles clamping the bivalves shut, allowing the shelfish inside to be snipped out, leisurely and neatly, and eaten.

3

Another medium-billed wader must be familiar to all birdwatchers as the strident sentinel of the marshes — the bird that gives you away by flying off yelping loudly and alerting all the birds in the neighbourhood to your presence. Such behaviour earned it in times past colloquial names like 'watchdog' or 'warden of the marshes' from angry wildfowlers deprived of their quarry. Redshanks have a habit of letting their strikingly bright red legs dangle as they hover, noisily scolding over some potential predator. By far their most conspicuous plumage feature at any season, however, is their flight pattern. The rump is white, and a broad white streak extends up the back between the wings, which are brown but with a very broad white bar running along the trailing edge.

Redshank

Near its nest on the saltings, the Redshank is a shy and restless bird, suspiciously bobbing both head and tail as it walks along, just as do the Common, Green and Wood Sandpipers, placed in the same genus and often to be seen at migration times beside the estuary creeks. Walking normally, the Redshank is slow and graceful, a feature that singles it out as it moves among the other waders on the mud. Although they are fairly numerous on most estuaries in winter, Redshanks rarely form large flocks and are more often to be seen dotted about in ones and twos, mixing freely with the other waders in an unusually cosmopolitan way.

Redshanks are among the few waders to remain on the estuary during the summer. They are early breeders, sometimes taking up territories as early as February in a mild winter. March eggs are not unusual in the south, and the season continues until late June or July. Most pairs are thought to be single-brooded each year, and this extended season is due to the replacement of clutches of eggs lost to predators such as crows, gulls and rats, or to natural disasters such as flooding by spring tides.

Inevitably, Redshanks' nests are well-concealed, built deep in the heart of a tussock of vegetation and thus raised slightly above generally damp surroundings. The leaves of the tussock arch overhead to conceal the nest and eggs from predators, and often the sitting bird will arrange the leaves around itself, once it has settled on the eggs, to act as an additional camouflage screen. There are usually four eggs, olive brown with darker speckles, sharply pointed and clustering neatly together in a square, blunt ends out, so that they nestle compactly beneath the sitting bird's brood-patch. The purpose of the sharply conical portion of the egg is to house the folded legs of the chick within the shell. This is important, as the young hatch with their legs well-developed, a thick covering of cryptically-coloured down, and with their eyes open. Unlike most small song birds, they run about and feed themselves as soon as they are dry. Normally each parent will keep watch over half the family as they feed and as they travel from one feeding ground to the next. They may walk or even swim some distance, the youngsters bobbing along buoyantly, propelled by their long-toed feet.

In autumn and winter, Redshanks may be joined on the estuary by Spotted Redshanks, their larger, paler and more elegantly slender cousins. Spotted Redshanks are noticeably longer in the leg, and lack that conspicuous white trailing edge to the wing. On many occasions, though, it is behaviour that gives the first clue to the relatively scarce Spotted Redshank's identity. The delicate rapid pecking feeding technique with a needle-fine beak is much the same, but the Spotted Redshank takes advantage of its longer legs and can often be seen wading out into the water, even until it comes half-way up its flanks. Its call, too, is characteristic: a sharp 'chew-it' instantly recognisable over the tuneful hubbub of other waders on the mud. Towards the end of spring passage, in May, some migrant Spotted Redshanks will be seen acquiring their splendid full breeding plumage. Then they are quite un-mistakeable and unlike any other wader, being sooty black all over, with a scattering of crescentic grey bars on the breast and flecked with white spots on the back. Against this the dark blood-red beak and legs are well set off, and the plumage as a whole gives rise to a commonly used alternative name, Dusky Redshank.

At the upper end of the size scale in both body size and beak length are the Godwits, Curlew and Whimbrel. Apart from a handful of Black-tailed Godwits breeding on British marshes, both Black-tailed and Bar-tailed are breeding birds of the Arctic tundra, as is the Whimbrel; whereas many of the

Black-tailed Godwit

Curlews wintering on our estuaries will be the breeding birds that help make our moorlands so melodiously exciting in the breeding season. Godwit beaks are long and straight, if anything slightly up-curved, and well suited to probing deep into soft mud for worms or small shellfish. So deeply will they probe that sometimes even their eyes submerge in the soft surface ooze, a tribute to the effectiveness of birds' 'nictitating membranes', a third eyelid that they possess which performs the function of a windscreen wiper. In contrast, both Curlew and Whimbrel have long down-curved beaks, again very well-adapted for extracting worms or shellfish from deep in their burrows. The Whimbrel is considerably smaller than the Curlew, with a brown and yellow striped head, and as it winters well to the south in equatorial Africa it visits our estuaries only on passage in spring and autumn. In contrast to the melodious yodelling of the Curlew, the Whimbrel has a staccato monotone whistle, repeated several times — hence its name 'seven whistler'. All four species have a delightful habit of tumbling down out of the sky on occasion when they arrive at their feeding grounds from their roost, a display of exuberance that has the delightful name 'whiffling'!

The sheltered waters of the estuary provide a haven for many species of wildfowl and the grebe family. Most geese only resort to the estuary when driven off their grazing areas on adjacent farmland or marshes, and even the

Brent Goose, now numerous on many of our estuaries, is no longer an estuary specialist. In the past, it was held that the Brent Goose and *Zostera*, the eel-grass, on which it feeds, were inseparable. Indeed, when *Zostera* beds were decimated by a disease, Brent Goose numbers plunged. However, the

Brent Geese

Zostera slowly recovered, and a series of mild summers in the Arctic saw Brent numbers rise at an explosive pace, so much so that much of the available *Zostera* was eaten by Christmas. The geese then turned their attention to winter wheat, which advances in farming technology and land drainage had conveniently placed just on the other side of the sea wall. Brent now favour wheat to such an extent as to be regarded as pests in some areas.

Among the ducks, Wigeon and Shelduck (the latter, with Mallard, being the only ducks to remain in any numbers on our estuaries to breed) are joined by the tiny Teal, elegant Pintail and slightly top-heavy-looking Shoveler in feeding by dabbling in the soft mud and shallow water for minute plant and animal foods. At high tide, or in the deeper creeks, the diving ducks will feed. One of the more widespread is the Goldeneye, with its larger angular head, bottle-green in the male, brown in the female. These are trying birds, as they seem to spend more time below the water than above it; getting a good view is difficult as they tend to drift with the tide, and predicting just where they are going to surface is almost impossible. Goldeneye are often joined by the fish-eating specialist ducks, the Goosander and Red-breasted Merganser. Though different in plumage, these two are very similar in build, with bristly crested heads, slender, elongated bodies for underwater streamlining, and narrow, serrated-edged beaks well adapted for holding slippery prey such as fish.

Goldeneye

Though lacking the special beak, the grebes too are predominantly fish-eaters. Many Great-crested Grebes and Dabchicks forsake their inland fresh-water breeding areas when these begin to freeze for the winter, and move to warmer sheltered estuarine waters. Here they may be joined by rarer relatives, the Red-necked Grebe (a little smaller than the Great-crested) and the Black-necked and Slavonian Grebes (both slightly larger than the Dabchick).

Most estuaries in industrialised countries, not just Britain and Ireland but the whole of Western Europe, have similar yearly patterns of bird visitors. These estuaries' main importance must be over the autumn and winter months, and some idea of this importance can be gathered from the sheer numbers of birds involved. The Waddensee in the Netherlands regularly holds

8

over half a million waders in autumn, with Oystercatcher, Knot and Dunlin each topping the 100,000 mark. In Britain, both the Wash and Morecambe Bay may hold in excess of 200,000 waders at peak times, with Oystercatcher, Knot and Dunlin again the most numerous species. It would be difficult to name an unimportant estuary bordering the North Sea or the Irish Sea. Even some of the apparently rather birdless estuaries of the south-west and western Ireland would seem to have real importance in severe winters. There is plentiful evidence from the results of ringing studies that many individual birds call routinely at the same estuaries each year on their way south, and should an estuary disappear, for all practical purposes, beneath a tide of industrialisation, the hazards to estuary birds would obviously be increased.

As autumn comes, the estuary gulleries and terneries will disperse, the adults taking with them the young raised on estuarine foods. Most birds, especially waders and ducks, will migrate to the warmer Mediterranean or to the tropical coasts of Africa. Some, like the Arctic Tern, will fly even further to the plankton-rich Antarctic Ocean. Some of the gulls, in contrast, will move inland, or remain on the estuary margins. In late summer and autumn, the times of peak passage movement, estuaries support a continually changing population of migrants, and it is probably to these birds that estuaries are of greatest value. Many of our winter waders have their major breeding areas on the Arctic tundra. Except for the natural hazards of changing weather, they are under little real threat either here or in their tropical wintering areas, so these 'staging posts' on our estuaries are vital. Not only do the stop-over areas allow recuperation from the flight from the north, but the birds also have time to feed and accumulate energy stores, mostly in the form of body fat, to serve as 'fuel' for the long journey ahead. Also, for most species the Arctic summer is too brief to do anything but raise a brood of young; the vital process of renewing the body and flight feathers in an annual moult must be postponed, often until the waders arrive on our estuaries in autumn. Therefore, again, any major loss of estuarine habitat could be disastrous.

With all these tasks to accomplish, and with the widely varying origins of the birds involved, autumn migration is spread out from early July, when failed breeding birds start to arrive back from the Arctic, through to late October or November. The transition from birds on passage to those remaining for the winter is not always easy to detect. Much depends on the severity of the onset of the Continental winter and the relative mildness of our own, but usually by December the estuary birds will be those likely to stay for the winter, unless forced to move south or west by freak winter conditions. Winter numbers, though still spectacular, are usually lower than autumn peaks, and of course the numbers of birds actually involved (bearing in mind the almost daily

9

arrivals and departures on autumn passage) over a period of time are considerably lower. Spring passage is a much more hurried affair. It begins in March and continues well into May, by which time many birds are giving us a glimpse — albeit brief — of their summer plumages, which are often remarkably colourful and in strong contrast to their winter drabness. The Arctic summer is so short that to arrive on the breeding grounds at its start and in good condition is of paramount importance; hence the apparent sense of urgency and the brief stays of the returning migrants on our estuaries.

What of the estuaries in summer? In late spring, the banks or islands will support some ducks and waders, but many, many, fewer than the autumn and winter populations, with only a few species involved as breeding birds, as most ducks and waders are primarily adapted to an Arctic or sub-Arctic breeding regime. However there will be terneries, usually of Common Terns in most estuaries, but occasionally of Arctic Terns in the far north of Britain. There will be gulleries, too, almost always of Black-headed Gulls which are the prime gull exploiters of the estuarine habitat.

A visit to a sizeable Black-headed Gullery is an experience in itself, impressive in that the entire population and the non-breeding 'loafers' rise to mob the intruder. Colonies begin to re-gather in March and April, as the gulls forsake their winter preferences for wide open spaces with a clear view of approaching predators for areas with sufficient ground cover to conceal nests and, more importantly, young. The whole performance of a colony is geared to massive mutual stimulation, from the choice of the actual colony site; the sudden 'dreads' when the birds rise as one in a wheeling, calling flock; to the onset of courtship and egg-laying. Because of this mutual stimulation, a remarkable degree of synchronisation in egg-laying and hatching is achieved, presumably to the overall good of the birds.

At the time of courtship, the chocolate brown hood, contrasting with the white neck and eye ring, has been found to be the vital centre, focusing visual attention during pair formation, and the ritualised head movements used in display serve to emphasise the contrast. Within the colony, males establish small territories, and strike an aggressive pose at the appearance of any other bird. This is followed by a 'stretching tall' posture, designed to make him appear as tall as possible, brown hood turned towards intruder, beak pointing downwards in defiance. Accompanying this are head movements ('flagging'), playing on the contrast between white nape and brown face as the head is suddenly turned sideways, presumably with a startling effect. Such measures will usually serve to frighten off a male intruder without actual strife, and serve to space out nests effectively to give the broods adequate space. The response of an intruding female differs: although partly frightened, she is driven on by greater sexual

They are usually seen singly or in pairs except when they have newly-fledged young, and many maintain their territories through the winter months. They are reluctant to cross the 'border' with adjacent territories, and will double back when reaching this invisible line. Usually their flight is low and bullet-like, with frequent penetrating 'zit . . . zit . . . zit' calls, generally over their home reach of water, though occasionally they will fly overland if alarmed.

Within the 'home reach' of water they also have a number of favoured boulders from which they hunt. These are often in midstream, and on them the Dipper stands, bobbing continuously. Against the background of broken white water, the apparent very conspicuous white bib can offer surprisingly good camouflage. As it bobs and dips its tail, it also blinks, using its so called 'third-eyelid' or nictitating membrane, which travels diagonally as it wipes the eye surface clean. In the Dipper, this nictitating membrane is conspicuously white, and underwater it is thought to protect the eye from gritty particles.

From the boulders in its stream, the Dipper will hunt, usually beneath the surface but occasionally just wading in the shallows. To submerge, the Dipper may jump straight into deep water or gradually walk into the stream until lost to sight. Once beneath the surface, it may hunt on foot, and this is where its disproportionately stout legs and powerful sharp-clawed starling-like feet serve a vital purpose in holding the buoyant body down on the stream bed. Under-water the wings may be used like a fish's fins both for propulsion and to maintain balance in strong currents, and sometimes they will swim for considerable distances. Hunting mission accomplished, the Dipper may walk out into the air again, or just bob up to the surface, where it can float buoyantly, often with wings partly spread. It may dive again, or if need be can take off from this position.

The breeding season begins early for the Dipper. The tunefully sweet, if slightly disjointed, wren-like warbling song can be heard in the territories from October onwards through the winter, until towards the end of the nesting period in the following June. Unusually, especially so as the plumages of male and female are so precisely similar, both sexes indulge in song with equal enthusiasm. In lowland territories, the first eggs are laid in early March, but up to a fortnight later in the Highlands.

The nest itself resembles a massive version of a wren's nest, built of dead grasses and moss. It is domed, with a side entrance, the dome often overhanging the entrance hole like a porch. In the past, most nests would have been in natural cavities in the banks of streams, or perched on a tree root exposed by flood waters. More recently, man-made sites have featured more, in buildings such as mills, or in weirs or dams. One of the commonest present-day sites is on the girders beneath bridges, where there is a secure foundation, shelter from the elements and good protection from predators. Such sites are traditional and may be used year after year.

Many nests are built behind natural waterfalls, and Dippers must be used to the almost annual hazards of sudden flooding endangering the nest and making the flight approach hazardous. In one case, fortunately observed and recorded in meticulous detail, their persistence in the face of adversity deserves special mention. The nest site was a natural one, in a river bank cavity, where the roots, grass and soil of the bank top had curled over, like a breaking wave, to give an overhang several inches away from the nest entrance and extending to a few inches below the nest. After torrential rains, the river rose in spate, until the floodwaters reached the top of the bank. The nest, fortunately, was safe from the waters, protected in the air-pocket held by the lip of the bank. It says much for the resourcefulness of the Dippers that, in keeping with their name, they dived under the turbulent waters to re-emerge in the air pocket carrying food to their young, which fledged successfully after the floods had receded.

Two other smaller birds may be mentioned here, which, although typical of the streamsides of the west and north, have proved themselves adaptable enough, or versatile enough in their diet, to penetrate into eastern and southern England where conditions allow. First of these is the Grey Wagtail, often confused with its summer-migrant cousin, the Yellow Wagtail. Though often found in damp meadows, the Yellow Wagtail is not a waterside bird. It is yellowish beneath and olive or buff above, whereas the longer-tailed Grey Wagtail has a grey head and back, and the yellow is limited to a brilliant lemon patch on the belly and beneath the tail. In the south-east, they offer salutory evidence to the birdwatcher of the benefits of being familiar with, and able to interpret, the Ordnance Survey maps. On these, mills, weirs, sluices and fords are marked, and it is to such places where the water is broken, clarified (and oxygenated) by these man-made structures, to the extent that it resembles a west-country stream that Grey Wagtails are attracted, and this is where the birdwatcher should head if he wishes to see one.

The second is the Siskin, one of the smallest of our finches. Other than conifers, the natural winter habitat of the Siskin is first among stands of mature silver birches, and later in the tops of alder trees lining the banks of rivers and streams. Though both Siskins and alders are more widespread to the west and north, alders do occur along some streams in eastern and southern lowland England, and in these, from dead of winter to early spring, small flocks of Siskins may be seen. They often feed in company with Redpolls, which are almost as tiny but brown and fawn (some with a red cap) as against the Siskin's yellows, greens and greys. They are seeking the alder seeds, which are carried within the alder cones which, like miniature wooden pineapples, are carried

18

in clusters at the extreme tips of flimsy branches. To reach them, the Siskin must use all the agility, and the ability to hang upside-down and feed, that we usually associate with the tit family.

In the lowlands in general, but the south-east in particular, the waterways are much murkier and the water moves much more sluggishly. As a result of this, there is a copious growth of a wide variety of water plants both on the river margins and in midstream which produces far more cover, and this in its train holds considerably more food items to suit a wider spectrum of diets than fast-flowing clear streams. In such dense vegetation, the slim body of the Moorhen is well suited to slipping between plants, while its long spidery toes support it as it crosses mud or floating vegetation just as well as do the similar feet of the tropical lily trotters. These long toes serve almost as well as webbed feet when

Moorhen

it comes to swimming, and the Moorhen is one of the most widespread of water birds, as much at home on a tiny pond in the corner of a field as it is in the vegetation beside a large lake. The copious vegetation provides plenty of nesting material, and most Moorhen nests are large piles of dead or decaying leaves, rising often a foot or more above the water. Because the nest is built on a rigid foundation — an overhanging branch or a clump of sedge or iris are the commonest sites — it remains susceptible to sudden rises in water level during flooding, whereas the shallower floating 'raft' nest of the Dabchick, although anchored to nearby vegetation, can rise and fall with the waters.

As they too are so numerous and often so tame, Mallard allow a close-up interest to be taken in their lives without seeming to be disturbed. So common are they, not just on streams and village ponds but on any stretch of water, even a park lake deep in the centre of a city, that it is tempting to assume that they are semi-domesticated. They seem dependent on man for liberal supplies of bread to keep body and soul together, but although it may be true that man is exploited by town-dwelling Mallard most are genuinely wild birds spending parts of the year in the remote open spaces of our rivers and estuaries, or migrating across northern Europe to distant breeding grounds.

Display starts before Christmas, the drake showing off his buffs and browns, curly black tail and bottle-green head to best advantage. He calls the female with an improbable-sounding whistle, and there may be excited chases on the water and in the air. When the duck is ready to mate, she signals this to the male by coyly bobbing her head to one side as she swims. Sometimes the weight of the drake as he mounts her submerges the duck entirely as mating takes place. Afterwards, the drake swims in a rapid circle round his female before both bathe vigorously. Once mating has taken place, the drake takes no further interest in the proceedings, and the duck becomes a 'one-parent family'. Her plumage, apparently so drab in comparison to her mate, is ideally suited to camouflage her for the long month she must spend incubating. Once they have hatched, many hazards face the young ducklings: swans, coots and moorhens — even other ducks — will take a peck at them if they come too close. Pike and large trout have them for a regular part of their diet, leaving only a tell-tale ripple to show where they were, and weirs and waterfalls wait to trap the unwary who stray too far from mother.

Much of the transport of agrochemical pollutants takes place through such lowland minor fresh waterways, where in addition may be located a range of industrial pollutants, some (like moth-proofing chemicals for carpets) more insidious than others, and industry may now be more of a problem than agriculture in this sense. Waterway pollution by persistent chemical residues has, in the recent past, been a factor implicated in a decline in numbers of the Heron, but despite this, and (as a bird dependent on open water for food) its vulnerability to extended periods of freezing winter weather, numbers now seem to be near normal.

Watching a single Heron pace sedately — even stealthily — round the edge of a lake in winter, always noiseless and often motionless as it looks for an unwary fish, it is difficult to believe what a noisily boisterous life Herons lead during the breeding season. Most of our Herons nest colonially in heronries, which may contain just a few or as many as a couple of hundred nests. Most heronries have been in existence for many years, some for centuries, like that at Chilham in Kent, which is noted in Kirkby's *Inquest*, a manuscript published in about 1290 in the region of Edward I. It is fascinating to see that almost 700 years ago in size and location it differed little from the present day.

Often the heronry will be in tall trees, but occasionally it is built in a reedbed, always within a short flight of a river or stream, or freshwater marsh, with dykes and drains, full of the fish, eels and frogs that are the Heron's main diet. This menu may be augmented by water voles, snakes and even duckling, moorhen or dabchick that carelessly stray within reach of the swiftly stabbing beak. As there may be as many as four or five nestlings, their parents have their work cut out keeping them fed, especially in large colonies, where they may have to fly a few miles to find a free stretch of water for fishing. The parents regurgitate a crop full of eels, fish and frogs (often not quite dead) into the bottom of the nest, adding a further gutteral dimension to the extraordinary cacophony of noise.

Kingfishers, too, are birds of placid, reed-fringed lakes or streams with plenty of overhanging vegetation, and with stretches of low earthen cliffs suitable for nesting. According to the ancients, the Kingfisher (called 'Halcyon') made a nest of fish bones and launched it on the sea. While she was brooding, the gods ordered that the oceans be calmed; this is the origin of the term 'halcyon days'. Actually, the nest could hardly differ more from the peace and beauty that are associated with the word halcyon. The nest is at the end of a tunnel up to a yard long, excavated by the birds in a suitable bank. In a chamber at the end lies the nest — made of fishbones, but dark, slimy, noisy and above all smelling powerfully of aged fish and the droppings of the young. So revolting is it that the parents often dunk themselves in the water immediately after leaving the tunnel to remove the scales and slime.

Often all that is seen of a Kingfisher is an electric-blue arrow, shooting past on whirring wings low over the water, jinking at the last minute to avoid over-hanging branches. Getting a good view of one perched becomes a matter of good fieldcraft, combining a stealthy approach with a good ear for the shrill 'ziii' call. A close-up view shows the basis of Gerard Manley Hopkins' statement 'As kingfishers catch fire', when the brilliantly iridescent blue back is suddenly turned away as the bird changes position, revealing the full glory of its bright chestnut breast and belly. A close-up view, too, allows inspection of the purposeful head and beak, disproportionately large compared to the body, and of the tiny blood-red feet, often so small that they are difficult to see. From such a perch, overlooking a favoured fishing place, Kingfishers wait and watch, the occasional bob of the head revealing more plainly the white half-collar. This is probably a gesture designed to alert other Kingfishers nearby, and warn them off its stretch of fishing water. Once a small fish is spotted, the Kingfisher will plunge, often submerging totally before emerging, almost vertically, shaking off water droplets and heading speedily for a good perch. There, with a few deft thwacks on the branch, the fish is stunned or killed and swallowed whole,

21

headfirst. The dive may often be at a shallow angle to a fish 20 or 30 feet (6-9 m) away, a tribute to the Kingfisher's keen eyesight.

Kingfishers are vulnerable not just to pollution, but to an excessive urge for tidiness and mechanical management on the part of man. Thus measures to 'improve' river banks by removing bushy vegetation and sloping the banks gently so that motor-mowers can be used, ostensibly introduced to improve

Kingfisher

drainage and reduce the risks of flooding, can hit a bird like the Kingfisher very hard. Although in themselves each of these incidents may have only a trivial impact on bird distribution or numbers, the long-term, cumulative effects are difficult to predict, especially as the regional water authorities have such sweeping powers covering such vast tracks of countryside. Aesthetically, a 'tidy' landscape with waterways devoid of fringing trees is undesirable enough, but ecologically the changes could be disastrous to a bird like the Marsh Warbler. This more melodious relative of the much commoner Reed and Sedge Warblers exists in a relic population in bushy, swampy areas in the west country. These swampy areas may be quite small, and are thus particularly vulnerable to 'tidying up'.

On the credit side, so far as industry is concerned, measures to counter pollution and improve the state of some major rivers have been strikingly successful. It is usually news of a salmon in the upper reaches of the Thames that makes the headlines, but recently there have been dramatic improvements too in waterfowl numbers and variety on the London reaches of the river. Most striking are increases in the numbers of diving duck such as Pochard and Tufted Duck, in dabbling ducks such as Teal, Shoveler, Shelduck and of course Mallard, and more surprisingly waders such as Dunlin and Ruff. All of these now feed in the grotesquely atypical surroundings of busy wharves and river traffic. Although chemically far cleaner, it is worth bearing in mind that the Thames is still relatively low in oxygen, and that the tiny bloodworm that forms the major food item for all these birds relishes such surroundings. Perhaps as the river becomes even cleaner, and better oxygenated, there will be a temporary drop in bird numbers as the bloodworms and the like die out and are replaced by a more typically river/estuarine fauna and flora.

In summer the lakes, or better lochs, of the Highlands of Scotland are often disappointingly barren. True, many will have Common Sandpipers breeding close to their shores, and a few will have the much rarer Wood Sandpiper breeding nearby. Very unusually for waders, some Wood Sandpipers will nest in trees, using the old nests of other species, usually thrushes. In the extreme west of Scotland, shallow lochs (especially on the sandy 'machair' of the Outer Hebrides) still hold a few pairs of Red-necked Phalarope. This, too, is one of

Wood Sandpiper

the exceptions to the avian rule in that it is the female which plays the dominant role in family life. It is she who is the brighter plumaged and larger in size, and who takes the lead in courtship displays. She does actually lay the eggs, but, this done, she leaves her drabber partner to incubate them and shoulder most of the burdens of feeding and caring for the growing brood.

23

Seen on the map, the Higlands (especially in the north-west) seem to be almost as much water as land, and it is here that birds seem few and far between. That said, once the birds have been found they can be spectacularly exciting. The small but beautiful Slavonian Grebe favours shallow, still, reed-fringed lochs, whereas Black-throated Divers prefer the wilder, deeper waters of the north-west. The closely related Red-throated Diver will make do with a pool in the peat the size of a garden pond, because it has a short take-off run and usually feeds in nearby sea lochs, but the Black-throated is heavier and needs a long take-off run. Because of this, and because it does most of its fishing in its nesting loch, it is the bird of the larger lochs. The population of Black-throated Divers is probably around 200 pairs, and the Red-throated probably less than 1000 pairs, so they cannot be thick on the ground nor necessarily easily found in such tough and roadless terrain.

Both birds, particularly the Black-throated, have elegant breeding season plumages but rather nondescript barking calls. The same cannot be said for the larger Great Northern Diver. Of all the bird calls in the world, that of the Great Northern Diver must rate as one of the fabulous and thrilling, echoing wildly between the mountains and across the lochs of its breeding grounds. The Americans call divers 'loons', and it is tempting to assume that this name comes from the maniacal laughing in the song, but a more likely derivation is from the Icelandic 'lomr' or loom, for lame or clumsy. A diver's body is well streamlined for successful underwater fishing, torpedo-shaped with the wings reduced in size. The feet are large, with lobed toes, and set back near the tail for best propulsion — hence their clumsiness on land. Divers only come ashore to struggle clumsily the few feet on to their nest, otherwise they spend most of their lives on the water.

The Great Northern Diver's nest is usually beside a large, lonely loch, although the birds may fly out to sea sometimes to feed. In Britain in summer, they are sadly exceedingly rare, with only a handful of breeding records in northern Scotland. The threat to these birds from egg-collectors is sadly all too real, even in the remotest parts of the Highlands. More often, Great Northern Divers will be seen during the winter, when the plumage is a much drabber variety of greys. Coastal waters, estuaries and, often, large reservoirs well-stocked with fish are all favoured localities.

Reservoirs in winter offer an excellent chance to watch the fishing techniques of all three divers. The hunting diver will patrol on the surface, often putting its head underwater to scan for fish. If it sights likely prey, it seems to slip under water, just sinking gradually from view leaving hardly a ripple, and once underwater it is a fast swimmer capable of staying submerged for about a minute.

Two species of wild swans visit Britain during the winter months, and often join with the Greylag and Pink-footed Geese on Scottish lochs. One, the Whooper Swan, matches our familiar Mute Swan in size (but is lighter in weight) and breeds in Arctic Russia and in Iceland, and it is usually these Icelandic birds that we see in Britain, most commonly in the west and north. The Bewick's Swan, which also breeds in Arctic Russia, is appreciably smaller and more goose-like than the other two, and occurs by suitable lakes and flooded meadows right across Britain. On land or water both wild swans carry their necks very straight, with the head at right-angles (rather like a walking stick), in contrast to the graceful S posture so typical of the Mute Swan.

The wild swans have the most wonderful trumpeting calls, audible for miles on a still day. These far-carrying calls have a vital function to perform when, often in deteriorating autumn weather, families of swans gather to migrate south. The overseas journey from Iceland to northern Scotland, for example, is about 600 miles (950 km) — many flying hours even on a swan's powerful wings and at a typical, wind-assisted, speed of about 75 mph (120 kph). Some of the journey may be made after dark, or in fog, and the calls will help to keep the flock together, preventing the inexperienced youngsters from getting lost on the way. They may even travel in cloud, as swans have been spotted on aircraft control radar migrating from Iceland at the staggering height of 26,000 feet (8,000 m): their identity and altitude were confirmed by the pilot of a passing aircraft!

As with the divers, it may be that the best views of wild swans for most bird-watchers will be achieved in manmade habitats in the lowlands of the south of England. Two of the best-known places for watching wild swans, Bewick's Swans in particular, are the wildfowl bird reserves of the Ouse Washes in Cambridgeshire (an area created by man originally to hold excessive winter flood water and so to prevent extensive flooding) and at the Wildfowl Trust headquarters at Slimbridge in Gloucestershire. Smaller winter herds occur annually at a number of widely scattered, well-grazed freshmarsh localities, as well as hill reservoirs and lakes.

Over much of England, but particularly in the south, the majority of pools and lakes are manmade, from tiny ponds in field corners created to water sheep and cattle through to huge reservoirs. Urban and industrial complexes demand water, and used to demand canals — hence we have reservoirs, and these today not just closely associated with urban areas, but also located in habitats varying from relatively flat arable farmland to remote, steep-sided valleys previously watered only by high rainfall and fast-flowing streams. Lowland reservoirs in particular are one good example of the winter value of such areas to bird populations. Taking London as an example, often as much as one half of the small British Smew population is to be found on the London reservoirs. Why this is the case for this small but supremely elegant fish-eating duck remains to be explained, but, as well as the rarer birds such as the divers already discussed, without question a very significant proportion of wildfowl wintering inland are supported by manmade waters.

Smew

Urban and industrial development also demands cement and concrete, and the extracted clay, chalk, sand and gravel to produce these construction materials. The winning of these minerals has resulted in widespread wet or swampy areas, possibly going some way towards replacing wetland lost to agricultural drainage, although still not providing adequate habitat for all of the species displaced. Perhaps more importantly, these new habitats can be designed and managed from the outset, or later 'converted' into nature reserves, or multi-purpose recreation areas where fishing and boating share, with nature, the addition to the landscape. However artificial, the provision of islands safe from disturbance and predators like foxes, or the creation of shallow beaches for feeding or resting, and a mixture of deep and shallow waters, may genuinely be better than the 'real thing'.

Something like three-quarters of the Little Ringed Plover population of 230 pairs in a 1967 census depended on these excavations for nest sites, and it seems that such mineral workings played a major role in this species' colonisation of Britain from the first nesting in the 1930s on the reservoir building site at Tring in Hertfordshire. Intriguingly, the larger and more domineering Ringed Plover (which usually wins territorial battles with its smaller cousin) is now venturing into this habitat from its usual coastal range, and to some extent is displacing the Little Ringed Plover.

Another summer bird of these waters (whose numbers on the same habitat in winter are augmented by Continental migrants) is the Great Crested Grebe. During the nineteenth century, countless grebes were slaughtered by man so that their plumage could be used to decorate ladies' hats, driving the species to the very brink of extinction. As a result of intensive lobbying in Parliament by worried naturalists, in 1870 the Great Crested Grebe became the focal point of the earliest bird-protection legislation, on which all subsequent protection acts have been founded. The grebe population, first censused at 2,700 adults in 1930, remained more or less at that level through the 1940s. The 1965 census showed an increase of 70 per cent to about 4,500, and it is presumably no coincidence that sand and ballast extraction increased by just over 80 per cent during the same period because of the post-war boom in building. Presumably, after the pressures of persecution had been released, the population stabilised at a level governed to a large extent by the availability of nesting territory.

Also associated with the increase in urban areas, but now of waning significance, was the development of rural sewage farms. Early sewage farms had extensive settling tanks, sludge beds and wet-meadow areas, each highly suitable for a number of wader species besides smaller birds such as Reed Buntings. As so many of them were situated inland, they produced valuable replacement or novel wetland that was swiftly exploited, particularly by migrants in spring and autumn. The invertebrate animal population of such a substrate was enormous, and clearly nutritious, so that migrants feeding undisturbed by tide cycles or other natural phenomena could quickly accumulate enough body fats to serve as stored energy to fuel the next leg of their migration. In this way, several waders like Little and Temminck's Stints, Green and Wood Sandpipers, Curlew Sandpipers and Ruff were introduced to apparently unlikely inland locations, and regular ringing operations showed that many birds took the same overland route at roughly the same time each year, calling at the same feeding places. With the change under modernisation programmes to more sophisticated techniques, where filter beds of clinker are all that are to be seen outdoors, this value to waders has disappeared and inland birdwatchers have lost many good sites. Filter beds do, though, provide feeding for birds such as starlings, and many new sewage farms seem to feed and house many Pied Wagtails in sheltered overnight roosts.

When we come to look at areas of predominantly waterlogged soil (call them marshes, swamps, bogs or what you will), the immediate reaction is that in the recent past — perhaps at most four centuries in the fens and much less in many areas — man by reclamation and drainage has amended British and Irish wetlands very considerably. Where the commercial pressures demanding a high return from every acre of land are less, as in areas of the extreme north and

27

west, the modification and 'up-grading' of poor wet land has been carried out on a correspondingly reduced scale. In all probability, the bulk of the impact comes from wet-meadow drainage, rather than from the loss of extensive reedbed areas that the conservationist and environmental ecologist prize so much today. Despite this, it remains true that birds like the Curlew and Redshank, typical of such areas, are still widely distributed today, breeding over much of these islands outside the south-eastern corner of England.

Unquestionably, small population pockets of a variety of specialist wetland birds will have been lost (the Marsh Harrier and the Ruff are good examples), but a highly subjective value judgement remains when trying to assess the relative merits of the wider range and probably greater numbers of birds inhabiting the replacement farmland. These losses are also offset by some intriguing (in the circumstances) gains. Savi's Warbler, for example, a reedbed specialist, has established a tenuous hold again as a breeding bird after an absence of about a century from eastern and south-eastern England. Another warbler, but from a different family and with very different habits, being non-migratory and preferring dank scrub and dense marshland vegetation, has performed very differently. Currently in an expanding phase in its Continental European range, since its first landfall in Britain in 1961 the Cetti's Warbler has gone from strength to strength in the south-east, apparently shrugging off unconcerned the adverse pressures of several severe winters that the pessimists thought would be this sedentary bird's undoing.

Even more paradoxical is the case of the Bearded Tit or Reedling. These delightful birds are very much dependent on the common reed, *Phragmites*, feeding on its seeds and nesting amongst its stems, and rarely venturing far from its shelter. On windy days, so feeble is their flight that they seem to fly amongst the reed stems, 'pinging' as they go, rather than risk exposure to the elements above them! The series of savage winters of the early 1940s reduced the breeding population to a mere handful of pairs by 1947 (two to four pairs in East Anglia were all that separated the species from extinction in England. Despite the concurrent loss of reedbed habitat, this tiny population flourished and reached 200—300 pairs by the 1960s, still confined to East Anglia. Then a series of eruptive autumn dispersions sent small parties to establish colonies in Essex and Kent, which have persisted and grown, and themselves 'seeded' new colonies nearby; and to other parts of England and Wales, where settlement has not been so permanent. At intervals since, some of our own birds plus some of the surplus population from the Dutch polders set out on these autumn movements, and despite their apparently poor flight capability and sedentary habits they may be seen almost anywhere in England and Wales, even in quite small *Phragmites* beds.

Perhaps the losses have been most conspicuous amongst the few British and Irish birds demanding really large reedbed areas in which to establish breeding territories. The Marsh Harrier is one such, which in addition to loss of habitat must also, as a daytime migrant, run the gauntlet of 'sportsmen' in southern Europe who find a slow- and low-flying bird an easier target for their shotguns

Bittern

than most. Though occasionally shot 'by mistake' (though one must wonder what for) the Bittern often overwinters in Britain and Ireland, and in consequence must face both loss of breeding habitat and the consequences of severe winters with the freeze-up of feeding waters that they bring. The Bittern, colloquially called 'bog bumper' because of its astonishing spring call, which sounds just like a distant foghorn, is one of the most specialist of reedbed birds.

Obviously its plumage of buff, brown and black streaks is ideally suited to camouflage in this habitat, but sheer cryptic colouration is reinforced by behaviour patterns. If disturbed, the normally plump Bittern, crouched in the reeds like a hunchbacked Heron, will shoot erect, long neck extended and streaked plumage paralleling the vertical streaks of the reed stems, and will remain upright and motionless until danger is passed. Like the related Heron, fish, frogs, eels and watervoles all feature in the Bittern's diet, as do many birds' eggs and young, including on occasion those of the Marsh Harrier, which builds a low reed platform nest in the same large reedbeds. This awful irony poses something of a difficult conundrum for the conservationist: which is he to favour by protection?

Wherever suitable swampy areas exist, other species seem well able to flourish. For example, Sedge Warblers are typical birds of the lush vegetation of wetland and waterside habitats. Sometimes they will encroach on the true reedbeds — primarily Reed Warbler territory — but more often they occupy the drier areas. Thus, although ancestrally birds of the swamps, they are adaptable to almost any luxuriant, slightly dank vegetation. Ginger-brown above, with heavy black streaking, rich yellow-buff below, with a dark crown and conspicuous pale eyestripe, Sedge Warblers are easily distinguished from their cousins, the Reed Warblers, which are an all-over unstreaked olive-brown, and tend far more to be birds of extensive reedbed areas. The songs of these two wetland warblers are sometimes difficult to separate: Sedge Warblers have a conspicuous, Whitethroat-like, song flight, but also sing from regular 'songpost' perches, often atop a bush. The song is a tumultuous jumble of phrases, some harsh, some twangy and some melodious. The Reed Warbler's song is far more repetitive, and contains many phrases mimicked from other marshland birds. Both are nocturnal migrants, the males arriving some days before the females and establishing territories. They sing a lot at night early in the season, which is thought to attract the attention of females migrating overhead.

The nest of the Sedge Warbler is well-hidden, normally situated low down in dense vegetation and far more difficult to find than the elegant basket-work structure of the Reed Warbler, neatly suspended halfway up the reed stems. Perhaps Cuckoos find the nests difficult to locate (or lay in) for although the Reed Warbler is one of the 'top three' Cuckoo foster-parents the Sedge Warbler is only occasionally parasitised.

In contrast to the Reed Warbler, which migrates south to tropical Africa in a series of relatively short stages, the Sedge Warbler is one of the most successful as a long-haul migrant. Sedge Warblers winter in swampy areas of tropical Africa, and just as astonishing as the navigational ability (that enables them to reach the same wintering marsh each year) is the mechanical ability of the bird as a flying machine. 'Fuel' for the journey is carried largely as fat deposited beneath the skin and in the body cavity. The Sedge Warbler weighs 12 g (½ oz) or so in normal trim; but, before departure south in autumn, it may feed up to such an extent that its weight exceeds 20 g (¾ oz). In this state the bird appears almost spherical, with fat deposited even under the eyelids. It has been estimated that enough 'fuel' is carried for between 60 and 90 hours of non-stop flying — certainly enough to reach Africa in one hop — and this is a striking tribute to the quality of wetland feeding.

If the Reed and Sedge Warblers are amongst the more demonstrative and noisily exuberant indicator species of wetland habitat, the Water Rail, though equally typical, is very different in its behaviour. It enjoys a somewhat undeserved reputation as one of the rarities amongst British and Irish birds; 'undeserved' because Water Rails were found in over one quarter of the 10-km (6-mile) squares of the Ordnance Survey National Grid (there are 3,862 of them) during breeding season surveys organised by the British Trust for Ornithology for the *Atlas of Breeding Birds in Britain and Ireland*. This was far more than most birdwatchers expected, and led to estimates of a breeding population of somewhere between 2000 and 4000 pairs, on a par with our Great Crested Grebe, Heron and Mute Swan populations!

To see a Water Rail well requires one or more of a number of factors to operate favourably: luck, which is probably as important as patience; a good hiding place overlooking suitable habitat; or a spell of really freezing weather extending over several days, which forces hungry rails out into the open to forage for food. The most startling thing to see is just how easily a Water Rail vanishes into nearby vegetation. This may often be dense-packed reed stems, yet the bird walks straight in, without a pause, like the fabled ghost walking through a wall. A close head-on view shows the origin of this ability, as the Water Rail is 'compressed laterally' (that is flattened from side to side); this constitutes adaptive evolution to its particular habitat.

For such a skulking bird, the Water Rail has an extremely raucous voice and an unusually distinctive (though certainly not attractive) range of high-decibel calls. The commonest call (and, once known, one of the best ways of locating Water Rails) starts off like the grunting of a pig and ends in a horrific series of squeals as if that pig were being slaughtered. Other calls include a staccato 'kek-kek-kek', which may be repeated monotonously long into the spring evening, interspersed with occasional dabchick-like whinnying trills.

Water Rails seem so attached to life on the ground (or occasionally on the water) that it comes as no surprise to see how small their wings are, nor to watch their feeble flight, legs trailing, fluttering low over the water. It is a surprise, though, to discover, from the results of ringing, that Water Rails are migrants, and often long-range migrants at that. There are many recoveries

31

showing a marked westerly or south-westerly immigration into Britain of Continental birds in autumn, and an easterly exodus in spring of birds ringed here during the winter months. Birds have been reported from as far afield as Sweden, Poland and Czechoslovakia.

Water Rails suffer during extremes of cold weather. They lose weight, and become more easily seen as they are driven out of seclusion. Normally, their diet is extremely varied, including a wide range of aquatic or wetland insects, spiders, shellfish, worms, crustaceans, amphibians, reptiles and small fish. They also take a wide range of plant roots, tubers, seeds and berries. In cold weather they may venture out onto stubble in search of grain, and also turn predator on any small bird that comes within reach of a swift dash and stab with their long beak: the range of victims includes Reed Buntings, Chaffinches and Wrens. The Water Rail, however, does not always escape unscathed: there are several records of Herons (which also come under pressure in freezing weather) catching, killing and eating unwary Water Rails as they emerge from the frost-rimmed reed beds in search of food — a clear case of 'the biter bit'!

In summary, while it is clear that drainage has played an important and beneficial part in the development towards self-sufficiency in Britain and Irish agriculture since the World War II, there must now be serious concern that it may be carried too far. Piecemeal or as a series of major schemes, drainage now threatens to destroy the remaining flood meadows and grazing marshes, particularly in England and Wales. Land drainage can have a catastrophic effect on the breeding habitat of birds as diverse as Snipe and Marsh Harrier, Shoveler and Yellow Wagtail. Similarly deprived of safe havens and a secure food supply are birds dependent on such habitats which spend the winter months in Britain and Ireland, including the Bewick's Swan, Wigeon and Pintail. Some species are now extinct in Britain as a result of drainage, others have declined to a dangerous level, and for most of the specialist wetland species in the lowlands of Britain survival may in the not too distant future depend on a relatively small number of suitably protected nature reserves. For birdwatching, this is a thrilling but threatened habitat.

3 The Changing Farmscape

One thousand years or so ago, much of Britain would have been forest-clad, with oak predominating, beech and ash on the chalk, lime and elm on some areas of heavier soil and alders in really wet areas. Over about 1000 feet (300 m) and on sandy soils in the south, lower in the north, Scots pine would have been the commonest tree. By Tudor times, large timber-framed houses were built to accommodate an increasing population, and the nation was in an aggressive mood that demanded a large wooden navy. Wood was then also a major fuel, both for domestic purposes and to support the first industrial revolution. An official report to Queen Elizabeth I commented that her forests were rapidly becoming 'utterly destroyed'. Further population increases, and the expansion of the industrial revolution proper, reduced forest cover to only about 5 per cent of the land surface during the nineteenth century.

Forest clearances were not, of course, solely to provide timber. They allowed (in fact were an inescapable part of) an expanded agricultural industry, aiming both to feed the growing population and to exploit export markets. The process of clearance produced, almost as an incidental consequence, a much more varied landscape than the original forests. Initially, the clearances would have been small and widely scattered, following the pattern of the 'dens' of the Kentish Weald, now reflected in village names such as Marden. The 'den' was a woodland clearing, used for crops and by livestock, often some distance from the homes it served: thus Tenterden was the den for Canterbury, some 25 miles (40 km) away.

Since mediaeval times, the clearances have extended and coalesced to produce today, over much of Britain, a network of copses and woodlands, linked by a still extensive (though diminishing) series of hedgerows. Even this hedgerow system has waxed and waned, with changing farming practice dictating large clearances followed by the enclosures (much hated at the time), when probably many of our present-day hedges were planted. Within this matrix crops are grown, and 'improved' agricultural land now covers above 70 per cent of the English landscape. The woodland/hedgerow matrix forms both a communication system and a reservoir for wildlife, plants and other animals, as well as birds, which can then exploit adjacent farmland.

What then has been the impact of these forest clearances on British birds? It seems likely that the nett effect has been a beneficial one, although there may well have been some reductions or even losses, notably of larger species like the Goshawk or the Honey Buzzard, which demand extensive forest areas for breeding. The effects can be likened to comparing the small bird populations of dense mature woodland with those of open forest glades: the latter may support twice as many birds of perhaps 50 per cent more species than the former. Obviously such figures cannot necessarily be applied to mediaeval or even earlier forest clearances, as ideas of both the composition of the forest avifauna and numbers of forest birds at that time must be purely speculative. That said, it seems very probable that many of the farmland species today were originally birds of the forest margins. Clearances for agriculture would have enhanced the status of many or most of these by vastly increasing the amount of 'forest edge equivalent', providing more space for nesting territories and more extensive, and diverse, feeding habitats.

Certainly the steadily accruing results of long-term census studies (like the British Trust for Ornithology Common Birds Census) would indicate that area for area farmland survey plots are generally richer than woodland and that more species occur exclusively on farmland than in woodland. Typical of the birds that flourish best in these circumstances is the Whitethroat, one of our summer visitor warblers. Although basically skulking, Whitethroats seem unable to resist the temptation to peek out at you inquisitively from deep cover, churring a warning to their neighbours as they do so. Early in the summer, when the males are devoting most of their energy to advertise and defend their territorial strip of hedge, they will shoot skywards over the bushes, hovering jerkily about while singing a few jaunty scratchy phrases before plunging head-long back into cover.

Until recently, Whitethroats were one of our most numerous summer migrants, but suddenly, in 1969, they were overtaken by calamity. Normal numbers left Britain in autumn 1968 for the wintering grounds in West Africa just south of the Sahara Desert. Here they live in a region of scrubland called the sahel, where the vegetation is adapted to, and tolerant of, periods of drought.

It is thought that a drought in the sahel, extending over several years before 1968 and causing much human suffering and loss of cattle, eventually impoverished the vegetation so much that the Whitethroats could not find enough food. The northward journey back across the Sahara is non-stop and formidable, and demands a rich food supply for some weeks beforehand for the Whitethroats to fatten up, the stored fat being used as 'fuel' on the journey. This was not available, so in spring 1969 only a few Whitethroats (perhaps 20-30 per cent of normal numbers) managed to return, the remainder perishing in the desert.

Fortunately, nature regularly demonstrates her basic robustness and made no exception of the Whitethroat. After a decade of first rarity, then scarcity, the 'happy ending' came as Whitethroat numbers began to increase again, and most of us on a summer farmland walk should not find it too difficult to locate the scratchy song of this attractive bird.

Yellowhammer

Perhaps the most typical of hedgerow birds is the Yellowhammer. Although never likely to be classed among the avian world's top songsters, it is because of its song — the jingle 'a little bit of bread and no cheese' — that most of us have known about Yellowhammers since early childhood. This wheezy song reflects the hay fever season through which the Yellowhammer sings—the long hot afternoons of high summer. Birds of open farmland like the Yellowhammer often choose conspicuous song posts such as bush tops, telephone wires or fence

35

posts. Good thick hedges are preferred in summer, but in winter they tend to flock with others of their kind and finches and sparrows in open fields, particularly around areas where sheep and cattle are fed hay, or in rough weedy ground or stubble, seeking seeds.

In winter, both male and female Yellowhammer are a drab yellowish fawn, with darker streaks and a few rusty red patches. In consequence they are very inconspicuous, as are the other seed eaters which needs must feed on the ground, as most seeds will have fallen by midwinter, so good camouflage is at a premium. What a change there is, however, as spring approaches. For camouflage purposes again, the female (which bears the brunt of incubation) retains her dull dress, but wear and tear will have worn away the buff and brown ends of the male's feathers, gradually revealing the breeding plumage beneath. Perched high on a song post in the sun, a male Yellowhammer for sheer colour will vie with the best of canaries so bright are his yellows and golds, rusts and chestnuts. It is all the more surprising, therefore, that we are taught about Yellowhammer song, not plumage. The gradual wearing of the feather ends to reveal summer colours has another neat adaptive purpose: the thicker the body feather layer the better the insulation properties, so this wearing will help to prevent overheating as temperatures rise in the warm summer weather.

Cousin to the Yellowhammer, and a bird of even more open farmscapes, is the aptly-named Corn Bunting. Although often associated with extensive fields of cereals, with skimpy hedges and only occasional song posts on the telephone wires, and also with the chalk ridges of the Downs and the Chilterns, its distribution is patchy, and it is difficult to understand why. The Corn Bunting is an enigmatic bird in many ways: it is extremely secretive, with its nest well concealed on the ground and the youngsters leaving the nest some days before they are old enough to fly, so we know relatively little about the breeding biology save that the males are sometimes polygamous, supporting several females and their broods. The Corn Bunting's plumage is amongst the least distinctive: both sexes look plumply overweight, and are grey-fawn with darker streaks all year round. Their song, though, fits into the 'once heard, never forgotten' category, and can tactfully be likened to the jangling of keys or, less elegantly, to small pieces of broken glass being shaken in a bucket!

Most farmland birds are characterised by a catholic choice of diet, and seem able to adapt quickly to new foods. The crow family in general exemplify this, and none better than the Magpie. The Magpie's diet is composed largely of small soil animals such as worms and various insects and their larvae, augmented by carrion, cereal seeds, fruit, berries and even the occasional unwary lizard, frog or small mouse. They extend their search for insects by looking for fly maggots and ticks in the fleece of sheep, and will often use 'sheep back' as a convenient

36

perch to scan the grass for insects, like grasshoppers disturbed by their mobile vantage point, down onto which they drop. In summer, they are notorious for their ravaging of small bird nests in the farmland hedgerows, each pair of Magpies systematically searching along all the hedges in their territory. This habit of eating any sort of bird or bird's egg including those of Pheasant and Partridge, has earned the Magpie great unpopularity with gamekeepers, and the present day distribution has been largely shaped by man. Since Victorian times they have been shot, trapped or poisoned (often using illegal means) and even today they are perhaps the commonest 'vermin' to be displayed on a game-keeper's gibbet.

With its omnivorous habits, which include secretive early-morning visits to garden bird tables and scavenging on town rubbish tips, the Magpie has shown itself well able to adapt to modern life. More than that, it is demonstrating the speed at which novel feeding techniques can spread through bird populations. The best known case is of Blue and Great Tits opening milk bottles, but now in the Midlands and North Magpies are demonstrating similar opportunism by following milkmen on their early morning rounds. They have learned to relate the milk float to deliveries of one of their favoured foods — eggs. No matter that the eggs arrive neatly packaged in cartons on the doorstep: the cartons are equally easily recognised and soon opened by the strong beak and the contents greedily eaten!

Magpies range over most farmland, showing some preference for rough grazing fields with thick unkempt hedges with taller trees suitable for building their football-sized domed nests of prickly twigs. They tend to avoid prairie farmland and treeless marshes, and shun equally tracts of dense woodland without any clearings.

There are, sadly, obvious examples where man has exerted too much influence on this 'typical' English landscape, this mosaic of fields, woods, copses, and hedgerows. Perhaps in most cases the cause has been an unreasoning and too religious a pursuit of higher profitability or productivity, although each of these must be amongst the legitimate goals for any farmer. The swing of the pendulum that enclosed with hedges the huge fields of a few hundred years ago has been reversed, and in some areas expanses of uniformity have reappeared, this time as the 'prairie farmlands' of extensive cereal monoculture. With the vital spinneys and hedgerows gone, and with an intensive spray programme of pesticides and herbicides reducing most other insects (not just the pest species) and most wild plants (not just the competitive weeds) to drastically low levels, such areas become almost uninhabitable.

The lethal nature of some of these chemical aids to farming has in some cases been tragically demonstrated by the widespread occurrence of poisoning amongst wildlife. Kills of Woodpigeons and unfortunately also of a bird with both economic and sporting value, the Pheasant, have been caused in the past by the birds eating spring-sown cereal seed dressed with an insecticide called dieldrin. More dramatically, a census of the Peregrine Falcon population showed

Pheasant

that the pre-war population of this magnificent bird of prey, of about 700 pairs, had been reduced to about 240 pairs by 1962. The breeding success of the remaining pairs had also declined alarmingly. Responsibility for this was laid at the door of DDT, an insecticide developed during the war years which was both extremely effective and cheap, and a genuine life-saver in eliminating mosquitoes from malarial areas. The great life span of such chemicals in the environment, and their property of steadily accumulating in the fatty tissues of the body, was not then understood. Peregrines, although apparently unlikely victims of poisoning by an insecticide, are at the top of a 'food chain', or 'food pyramid', and accumulated harmful or sometimes lethal doses from the bodies of the various birds that formed their prey. Far more is now known of the details of pesticide potency, persistence and mode of action, and voluntary constraints on use are in force and a detailed series of tests, including environmental impact, must be undergone before a new material is released. Peregrine numbers are now — twenty years later — on the increase again, but this heartening state-ment needs to be regarded with some caution. Although we have a better understanding of pesticides, still relatively little is known about the potential impact of fertilisers (especially by running-off into waterways) and herbicides. Chemical weed control is a fast-expanding market, and although many of the materials are not in themselves poisonous to animal life, the potential long-term ecological impact of the removal of food stocks may be alarmingly greater than anticipated. There are some indications that extensive herbicide usage although solving some problems for the farmer may be helping to create others. With the steady reduction in naturally-available seeds as a food resource, is it too surprising to record an increase in the removal of the seeds from strawberry fruits by Linnets? In some areas, this problem is entering a new, even more sophisticated phase: the introduction of polythene tunnel cloches has produced even earlier crops, which provide a readily available food source at the time of greatest natural seed scarcity. Linnets have 'discovered' the crop under the polythene, and are enjoying the food as well as the insulation that the tunnels provide from both the elements and any bird-scaring devices that the grower may employ!

In orchard areas also, recent years have seen the removal of considerable mileage of hedgerow and with it a broad spectrum of food plants. In many places, the old mixed hedges have been replaced with windbreaks of alder, and it is possible that this too may bring problems in its train. Redpolls are amongst the smallest and most charming of farmland birds, and usually feed on weed seeds in stubble and fallow fields. Redpolls, which are subject to erratic population fluctuations, are often found in orchards and can cause damage by eating opening blossoms and fruitlets. The seeds of alder are a major natural food of the Redpoll, and we may wonder whether these new windbreaks are playing a part in the present upsurge in Redpoll numbers. Are farmers creating a problem for the future by spreading this food resource, attracting Redpolls to orchards where, when the supply of alder seeds runs out, buds and fruitlets are readily available?

Subtler changes on the farm, on the face of it unlikely to have much impact on birds, may sometimes have a disproportionately large effect. Barn Owls, already prone to high mortality during severe winter weather because of the difficulties they experience hunting their rodent prey (which lives on happily in the vegetation beneath the snow), and prone also to high mortality due to pesticide contamination because of their position at the top of a food chain, serve as an excellent example of this. As its name implies, the Barn Owl is the most farmland-specialist of the owl family, depending heavily on small rodents (many of which may cause agricultural damage) for food. For nest sites it uses old, hollow hedgerow trees and (again as its name suggests) rarely-used or derelict farm buildings, and it is here that the subtle effects come into play. Dead trees are often removed in the cause of hygiene, or in the interests of safety.

39

or in the process of hedgerow removal. Old, perhaps slightly tumbledown and certainly dark, barns are demolished to make way for far more efficient and practical, light and airy corrugated asbestos replacements, which do not offer Barn Owls the peace and seclusion they need to breed successfully. With all these factors against them, it is particularly heartening that the farming community

Barn Owl

has readily recognised the ecological and aesthetic role of the Barn Owl, and in many areas new farm buildings are fitted with simply-constructed nest boxes, sited in a quiet corner and often provided with a special entrance hole, to help counter the adverse pressures. It is to be hoped that the general decline of the Barn Owl will be arrested.

The scarcity of hedges in which to shelter, find food and nest, and along which many small animals and birds (despite their powers of flight) will move, automatically eliminates most small birds from prairie farming regions. Their lines of communication are hopelessly broken. Were there to be more insects within the crop, however (not pest species of course), and just a few hedgerows left to provide shelter for nests and further supplies of insect food, large fields could be ideal Partridge country. Though spending much of their lives feeding on plant material and seeds, young Partridges need the high protein content of insect food in the early stages of their lives, when growth is most rapid. Too 'clean' a crop, and the Partridge chicks will starve, or succumb to a short spell of bad weather, as they spend more energy walking about the cereal fields looking for food than they gain when they eventually do find the odd insect.

Related to the Partridge, but very much restricted to the south-east of England, particularly on the chalk, is the Quail. So well camouflaged is the Quail that the most to be hoped for is a fleeting glimpse, but on warm after-

Partridge

noons in suitable areas (and in suitable years, for Quail are migrants and very scarce indeed in some summers) their 'wet-my-lips' call can be heard. Even this is tantalising, as Quail have astonishing ventriloquial powers, and pinpointing the calling birds is exceedingly difficult.

If Quail are exceedingly difficult to find, Skylarks are quite the opposite. They, too, favour areas with large fields but seem also to flourish fairly well both in areas of intensive pesticide and herbicide usage, and in the west where fields in general are far smaller. The Skylark is a ground nester; the streaky browns, greys and buffs of its plumage conceal the sitting bird extremely well on its dried grass nest against the background of the soil. The sitting bird sits tight, so tight that you almost need to tread on the nest to dislodge her. The nestlings are well camouflaged too, and leave the nest early, a few days before they can fly. Once away from the nest, the family splits up and the youngsters hide singly over a wide area. This gives them a much better chance of escaping the attentions of predators such as foxes and weasels.

Contrary to popular belief, Skylarks quite commonly sing from fence posts, or even from a large lump of earth on the ground, and here it is possible to see their unexpectedly large and conspicuous crest, raised in song. It is often said

41

that this 'ground song' is different from the normal, but if it exists this difference is too subtle to be easily detected. No noise can surely be more typical, more redolent, of the open countryside in summer than the song of the Skylark. The songster may often be difficult to find when singing several hundred feet up, though this is not quite 'at Heaven's gate' as Shakespeare would have us believe. The male Skylark is setting his traditional boundary markers with these bursts of song, and it is worth watching to see how precisely he can locate and maintain his station, hovering on quickly-beating wings with tail fanned, bobbing about as if attached to the sky by a length of elastic.

By no means so well able to keep abreast of the changes in its preferred habitat being brought about by changing farming techniques is the Green Woodpecker. The Green Woodpecker is the largest of the British woodpeckers, and paradoxically spends much of its time on the ground rather than pecking wood. What it is doing is looking for ants, and probably one of the major reasons for its scarcity now, as compared with as recently as twenty years ago, is not so much that it suffers during severe winters but more that grassland, in general, has been so much 'improved'. The classical habitat of Green Wood-peckers was short-grass meadows, kept cropped by intensive sheep raising or by rabbits and lumpy with numerous ant hills. Myxomatosis drastically reduced rabbit numbers, and faster-growing regularly fertilised grasses which are mown by forage harvesters and stored for winter feeding demand that the anthills be removed. This may be by the regular cultivation that modern grassland, like other crops, now receives, or it may be that physical removal is necessary to avoid damage to the mowing machines.

This is sad, as there is a tendency to compare our birds unfavourably with those highly-coloured species from tropical areas, and few tropical birds can compete with the vivid beauty of the Green Woodpecker. Often the first view is of a pigeon-sized bird, apparently made of pale gold, crossing the meadows in deeply undulating flight. A closer view gives the full beauty of the greens and golds, set off by a scarlet cap and black, white and scarlet moustaches, quite unexpected on a British bird.

Ants and their larvae, and various other insect grubs, are collected on the Green Woodpecker's tongue, which is a masterpiece of evolutionary adaptation. As in all woodpeckers, it is surprisingly long: it can protrude for three or four inches (8-10 cm), and when not in active use lies coiled in a tubular sheath running beneath the lower jaw, up the back of the neck and onto the top of the skull. This long tongue can be inserted into ant runs, and is covered in copious quantities of a very sticky saliva, to which the ants adhere, to be eaten as the tongue is withdrawn.

With the range of adaptability and versatility in diet that occurs amongst

Skylark

forest-margin birds, it is hardly surprising that some of them have seized the chance to turn their attention to our crops, in the process becoming 'pests' in our eyes. Perhaps it is even less surprising when we consider that most cultivated crops are derived from wild ancestors that feature naturally in bird's diets, and that the principal aim of the plant breeder has been to make the fruits of his cultivars bigger and better than their progenitors, and thus presumably easier and better feeding for avian pests.

Often, however, if agricultural bird pest problems are examined in any detail, their origins seem to be man-made. Had we not, for example, changed our farming system so that clover-rich meadows became redundant in the modern context and vanished, the Woodpigeon would not have been 'forced' to turn its attention to our brassica crops. In fact cabbages, brussels sprouts and the like are only a subsistence diet for Woodpigeons, far from being a favourite food eagerly sought after. Watch Woodpigeons flighting in to roost in woodland after a day feeding on brassicas: their crops are bulging to bursting point, giving them a very top-heavy appearance (like a jumbo jet) in flight. Because the food value of brassica leaves is so low compared with the clover stolons and shoots of their preferred diet, Woodpigeons must go to roost with a full crop to digest during the night to produce enough energy — in the form of body warmth — to enable them to survive the long cold hours of midwinter darkness until, at first light, off they must go again to begin another day of ceaseless feeding. No wonder damage is so great both in terms of crop actually eaten and that spoiled by the birds' droppings.

The Woodpigeon is often a serious pest, and has few admirers, but the Bullfinch is rather different and very much a case of 'beauty or beast?'. Most people, including gardeners and farmers, would agree that the Bullfinch is strikingly beautiful, the male grey-backed, scarlet-breasted and black-capped, the female a subtle mixture of suede browns. Let no one doubt, though, the other side of the Bullfinch character. Beneath that black cap is a sharp, slightly hooked beak, rounder in profile than most finches. This is ideal for nipping off whole buds from trees and shrubs and biting out the core. This process can be so fast that apple and pear buds are eaten at ten per minute, blackcurrant and gooseberry buds at the staggering rate of thirty per minute!

Surveying the wreckage after a period of Bullfinch attack, many fruit growers see so many bud fragments scattered about that they make the assumption (natural enough) that nothing has been eaten and that the attack was sheer wanton vandalism. This is far from true, as the attack on the buds has been both technically skilful and purposeful. In the heart of the bud is set

Bullfinch

the 'flower initial' which ultimately grows into the flower or flower cluster. In the case of a pear bud, which in midwinter is about the size of a small pea, this flower initial is a little larger than a pin head and looks like a small cauliflower. Here much of the 'goodness' (in nutritional terms) of the bud is concentrated, and it is this that the Bullfinches are seeking when they discard the bulky residue of the protective scales and leaf initials of the bud to feed as efficiently as possible.

For most, or, in the case of all Bullfinches living outside fruit-growing areas, for all of the year, their diet is a mixture of wild natural foods. In summer, the emphasis is on the seeds of dandelion, buttercup, stitchwort and many other plants, shifting to nettle in late summer and dock in autumn and early winter. As winter sets in in earnest, most seeds fall to the ground, but dock and bramble seeds remain on their parent plants and readily available to Bullfinches. After Christmas, these seeds are supplemented by ash keys, until, later in winter, the buds of blackthorn and hawthorn are taken. Most Bullfinches will survive perfectly well all their lives on this natural diet, and it seems that only when natural supplies fail for some reason will those birds resident close to gardens or orchards turn their attention to cultivated varieties. When they do, they find such a palatable alternative that the forthcoming season's blossom (and thus in the case of fruit, the crop too) is almost destroyed.

Bullfinches damage most severely those orchards planted right alongside their preferred woodland habitat; orchards distant from woods escape un-scathed. The message should be clear enough, but since the time of the first Queen Elizabeth the Bullfinch has been a bird with a price on its head. Chroniclers of the time note that one penny reward was offered for 'everie Bulfynche or other Byrde that devoureth the blowthe of fruit'. For other birds often labelled as farm pests, the message (when examined closely) is not so clear. There is no denying that flocks of freshly-fledged juvenile Starlings can do a great deal of damage to the crop in a cherry orchard in remarkably rapid time — a parallel to the human 'teenagers on the rampage' — nor that they can damage early apples. In winter, our own Starlings are joined by massive flocks of migrants from Europe, and in some cases winter feeding flocks cause problems by descending in hordes on the food set out for calves being reared in barns. What of the other side of Starling activity? It is relatively easy to cost the damage they do, but much more difficult to assess the benefits that they bring by eating the damaging larvae of a number of soil insect pests. By far the commonest sight of Starlings on farmland is flocks busily probing in grassland, so the beneficial aspects of Starlings might be considerable.

It has long been a puzzle why Rooks tend to be regarded as a pest in Scotland, and either as an 'ordinary' farmland bird or occasionally as a game bird for shooting in England. The answer seems to lie not as might be imagined in differ-ences in Rook numbers between the two countries, but in the relative sowing dates of cereal crops. In the north, sowing tends to be late in spring and coincides with the Rook's breeding season, feeding on the cereal seed satisfying their high energy and protein demands at this time. In the south, the milder climate allows the earlier-sown grain to grow away too quickly, so the Rooks are denied it as a food source. However, maize is recently beginning to feature as a crop in those areas of southern England climatically suited to its cultivation. Maize requires relatively high soil temperatures to germinate and because of this must be a late-sown crop. Thus it is proving vulnerable to Rook attack.

Rooks are very much a feature of the farmscape in Britain and Ireland. On any fine day from midwinter onwards, especially if there is a fresh breeze, the birds will be seen over their rookery, throwing themselves about in the sky in an aerobatic spectacular. Although much of this aerial cavorting may be prosaically linked with pair formation and display for the coming breeding season, or with learning and developing flying skills, it is difficult to dismiss the idea that some element of sheer enjoyment is involved, so recklessly enthusiastic do they seem. The rookery itself is a township in the sky, with its own community structure, as complex as a human community and, like them, with its social problems. Older pairs of Rooks will nest in the safer sites, in substantial branches near the centre of the colony, the nests growing bulky as twigs accumulate over the years. Younger birds, the 'newly-weds', are relegated to the fringes of the colony, often building fragile nests amongst the slender topmost twigs in the trees and thus liable to be overtaken by disaster. Rooks are aggressively possessive of their nest site and the twigs of which the nest is made, but the minute a back is turned petty thieving of twigs occurs, ensuring that the rookery is in perpetual turmoil and there is a cacophony of noise as birds argue with their neighbours.

Usually the rookery is built in the tallest trees around, sometimes in town or village parks or churchyards, but characteristically in farmland spinneys or hedgerows. An old adage suggesting that Rooks will desert dead or dying trees has more than a grain of truth in it. This has been evidenced during the recent epidemic of dutch elm disease, which has so dramatically amended the visual aspect of the lowland landscape as trees fall or are felled. In some areas, Rook numbers have dropped appreciably as a consequence, and there have been many cases of local removal of elm rookeries to sound trees — oak, ash, beech or conifer. Rooks enjoy feeding on freshly sown peas as well as grain, but as with Starlings some at least of this damage is alleviated by the amount of time that Rooks spend probing in soft fields for damaging soil pests such as leatherjackets.

Across Britain and Ireland as a whole, the nature of the farmland naturally changes quite dramatically. Climate, particularly the higher rainfall and warmer winters of the West Country or the colder winters of the north, plays a major part in this, as does altitude. Britain and Ireland are as diverse agriculturally as they are scenically, and the landscape is very much a patchwork quilt of crops with no single crop or type of farming exclusively dominating the scene for hundreds of miles at a stretch as is the case in parts of North America. Thus any descriptions of a farming type in the various regions must be a broad generalisation: nowhere will it hold true for long, and this surely adds to the attractions of farmland birdwatching, as the greater the diversity of farming activities the broader the range of birds which are likely to be encountered.

In the north of Britain, grassland and rough grazing predominate, with more waders and wetland birds like Reed Buntings to be seen on a farmland walk than in the south. Even in northern Scotland, however, on the east coast there are considerable arable farmland areas, and around the River Tay extensive soft fruit plantations. Generally speaking, the higher the altitude and the poorer the grazing, fewer birds will be seen of fewer species, and the impoverishing effects of cold winter weather will be the more marked. The west of Britain, and Ireland, have a predominantly grassland agriculture, but by no means are they exclusively stock or dairy areas. Fields are smaller and hedgerows better developed than in the Midlands and eastern England, but despite this the range of species to be seen is on the whole lower than in the east except in arable and fruit growing areas. Waders and waterfowl seem to be more prominent here than in the east, as do Ravens, Chough, Buzzards, Sparrowhawks and the chat family — Stonechat, Whinchat and Wheatear. The greatest diversity of farmland birds is to be found in the south, east and Midlands of England, where the climate is favourable overall and the farming diversity greatest.

So farmland birdwatching is within easy reach of most of us. The range of birds involved is wide, and numbers are often high in both summer and winter. Their adaptations to farmland life are fascinating to observe, even in those species that we regard as pests. Despite the striking changes in the practices and patterns of agriculture in recent years, there is in this diversity of birds an ample demonstration of the resilience of bird populations, and of the continuing rewards of farmland birdwatching.

4 To the Woods

In no habitat is the influence of man and his urban, industrial and agricultural expansion more dramatically evident than in woodland. Even a thousand years ago (a very short time in bird evolution terms) much of our landscape would have been covered in extensive tracts of native hardwood trees, with our only native conifer, the pine, similarly widespread on sandy or upland soils. Today, this forest cover (variously estimated then at 60-80 per cent of the land surface) has been reduced to a very piecemeal 10 per cent or less, despite recent deliberate emphasis on re-afforestation schemes. In addition, particularly in the case of conifers much of the new planting is of alien species, introduced for their plantation timber qualities from several parts of the world, and often these species are sited in areas that would naturally have supported deciduous trees. In the previous chapter we have seen how farmland birds in general have exploited this change successfully, despite the fact that most seem originally to have been forest birds. So what of the forest birds themselves: how have they fared?

Some areas of primeval coniferous forest remain, notably the Caledonian pinewoods of the Spey Valley and other localities in the Highlands of Scotland. Within this living antique of a forest, under serious threat of extinction by the pressures to introduce commercially viable conifer plantations to replace it, widely-distributed woodland birds such as the Chaffinch flourish, as do conifer-preferring species such as the Coal Tit. Two species, however, make this specially their home — the Crested Tit and the Scottish Pine Crossbill. Nowhere are Crested Tit numerous, and the total population in Scotland may be only just in excess of 1000 pairs. With its stuttering trill of a call, conspicuous crest and bold black-and-white face pattern, the Crested Tit is not easily overlooked where it is present. The strange part is that it is not far more widely found. Of all the tits, it seems the best adapted to life in coniferous woods, even being capable (as a normal routine) of excavating its own nest hole, and in Continental Europe it is very widely distributed in a variety of conifer types stretching from the Mediterranean coasts north to Scandinavia. It is, though, extremely sedentary, and it may be that its limited range in Scotland is a reflection of the reduced state of its ancestral home forests, to which it has become closely adapted over the ages, and that its lack of mobility prevents the colonisation of the 'new' conifer forests in England by immigrants from over the Channel.

The Scottish Pine Crossbill is another example of close adaptation to a particular tree species, not just habitat type. In the Northern Hemisphere, the woody cones of the various native conifers — larch, spruce and pine — are exploited by a very specialised family of birds capable of extracting the seeds from between the rigid wooden 'flakes' of the cones. In Scandinavia and to the east, it is the Two-barred Crossbill that specialises in the small, relatively flexible cones of the larch and the Common Crossbill that tackles the cones of spruce, which are rather larger and tougher. In keeping with the job they have to do, the beaks of these two birds differ in size and thus strength, though retaining the same flattened, cross-tipped profile that allows them to snip out the seeds from the cones with ease and which gives the family its name. Largest of all is the Parrot Crossbill, capable of dealing with the massive cones of European pines; but only slightly smaller is the Scottish Pine Crossbill, adapted by long isolation to feeding from the cones of the Scots pine. Interestingly, the Scottish Pine Crossbill, like the Crested Tit, is sedentary and rarely, if ever, seen outside the Caledonian forest; but other crossbills — the Common Crossbill of Europe — are regularly seen elsewhere in Britain, occasionally breeding in southern conifer plantations in considerable numbers.

The Common Crossbill has evolved a migration stratagem that assists its survival when food becomes scarce. This normally occurs after a series of good breeding seasons on the Continent, when numbers are high and pressures increase on the remaining stocks of cones. After the breeding season, many birds move away west, sometimes not travelling far before adequate food is found, but at other times moving in numbers across the Channel and settling in the 'new' forests of south and east England.

Because they feed in the tops of tall mature cone-bearing conifers, which are evergreen and carry long 'needle' leaves, and because many of the birds are females or young and thus yellowish or greenish brown in colour, getting a good view of Crossbills at work may not always be easy, but is well worthwhile. They have a parrot-like heavy-headed appearance and also a parrot-like agility as they reach towards a new cone, often hanging upside down. They are relatively quiet when feeding, although using an explosive 'chip' flight call, but one give-away that Crossbills are about overhead is the occasional dropping of partially eaten, slightly shredded cones to the forest floor. Interestingly, their nesting season is geared more to the availability of good supplies of suitable food than to our concept of 'the seasons'. In consequence Crossbills — particularly

Crossbills

Common Crossbills in England and lowland Scotland — may often breed very early, sometimes sitting on eggs in late November or December, with snow lying on the back of the incubating female! Most clutches in the south are laid in February and March, and in the Caledonian Forest the Scottish Pine Crossbill lays in March and April.

Until a few years ago it was fashionable to condemn mature conifer plant-ations that were alien either because of the species used or because of their location as being virtually birdless. The trees were planted so close that even the rides between plantation blocks seemed like grey canyons, muffling all sounds save the sighing of the wind. It seemed that Woodpigeons, Coal Tits and Chaffinches were the major avian inhabitants, and these only in low numbers. As more and more of these plantations are explored (and the paths in many are open freely to the public) attitudes are changing, and there is support for the changing view from detailed census work throughout Britain and Ireland. There is now plenty of evidence that, even when mature, conifer plantations may be a perfectly serviceable habitat, carrying reasonable numbers of a fair diversity of species including thrushes, warblers, tits, birds of prey and owls. There are, too, particular attractions such as the Crossbill, which has been joined in recent years by the Firecrest as a bird worthy of special pilgrimage.

The Firecrest shares with its close relative the Goldcrest the distinction of being the smallest bird resident in Britain and Ireland, with an overall length of just over 3 inches (7.5 cm) and weighing in at about six to the ounce (28 g). The Firecrest has all the rotund charm and delicacy of its commoner cousin, but with an elegant bronzy mantle and a most distinctive black and white stripe pattern through the eye making identification reasonably easy. Not long ago, Firecrests

Firecrest

were scarce passage migrants, much sought-after by birdwatchers at a handful of coastal bird observatories in early spring. In 1962, in the New Forest in Hampshire, freshly-fledged young were seen, and in the twenty years since small colonies have been established there and in several other countries in southern, central and eastern England. It is more than likely that breeding Firecrests may still be overlooked, as it is difficult to get good views of them as they flit about high in the evergreen canopy, and many of the early breeding

51

records were from plantations of Norway spruce (the 'Christmas tree'), at the time a habitat shunned by most birdwatchers.

Goldcrests and Firecrests have remarkably similar breeding biologies, although the former, as a long-established conifer specialist, is much more widespread and often very numerous. The nest is usually well hidden in thick foliage towards the end of a branch, and is one of the neatest constructed by any bird. It is a tiny basket of moss, held together with strands of cobweb and suspended, hammock-like, beneath the angle between two branches. In this the eight or more eggs (obviously lightweight) are easily contained, but the cobweb suspension proves quite capable of supporting the full-grown brood of young and their parents.

Goldcrests are perhaps *the* typical birds of coniferous woodland in Britain and Ireland, no matter how densely the trees are planted nor how 'commercial' the management of the plantation. The song is a high-pitched 'deedly-deedly-dee' with a terminal flourish. As the eardrums age and harden, so man's hearing of high-pitched songs fails, and the Goldcrest's song is so high-pitched that bird-watchers can supposedly assess their age, and the acuity of their hearing, by listening for them. In parts of eastern England, where conifers are scarce, Gold-crests are often found in churchyard yews or in well-grown ornamental conifers in parks and gardens. Populations in deciduous woods are normally much smaller, but after a succession of mild winters (severe cold or heavy snow hit the Goldcrest hard) the population tends to 'explode', and even lowland oakwoods will support fair numbers.

When feeding, Goldcrests (and Firecrests too) are forever active, restlessly flitting here and there among the twigs, peering into buds, hanging upside-down to inspect the undersides of leaves for aphids, and occasionally hovering, flycatcher-like, to snap up some small flying insect. Much of their diet is small insects, mites and spiders, and their eggs or larvae, sought out in their hiding places in cracks in the bark and extracted with the needle-fine beak tip.

One great benefit of modern conifer forestry to bird populations is that it is a managed enterprise, with the trees being regarded as a crop, and thus a rotation ensues, normally on a time scale of 40-80 years. Thus in any sizeable forestry area there will be plantation blocks of widely varying ages, each suiting different types of birds. Those felled within the past year may, if a few deciduous trees remain (as is often the case, especially in the south), be suitable for attractive birds like the Tree Pipit, with its parachuting descending song flight, and the now-scarce Nightjar, which is otherwise largely confined to sandy heaths. The Nightjar, and its nest and eggs, are amongst the most perfectly camouflaged of all natural things. Commonly Nightjars choose as a nest site the burnt area around a bonfire used to destroy the smaller branches remaining after felling, and even at a range of only a few feet the sitting bird or the exposed eggs are astonishingly difficult to discern.

The value of plantations in their first decade or so cannot be underestimated, nor can their potential as birdwatching sites. Several species owe both their numerical strength and their wide distribution today largely to the existence of such areas, even in central and southern England. A good example would be the Hen Harrier, which succeeds well in such areas in the west and north, but others may seem more surprising. Despite the fact that many new plantations may be in quite dry localities, two supposedly wetland species, the Grasshopper Warbler (with its 'perpetual fishing reel' song) and the Reed Bunting both flourish in them. As they age, these plantations become suitable first for scrub-loving birds like the Yellowhammer and (in the west) the Whinchat, then for birds like Chaffinches, Coal Tits and Goldcrests, until they reach fruiting age when they become acceptable habitat for specialists like the Crossbill as well.

Hen Harrier

In deciduous woodland, too, the physical structure of the wood plays a significant part in determining the sorts of birds that are likely to be seen. This physical structure is today often a direct result of management policy, but there are still many areas of semi-natural woodland where nature plays the major role in determining where there are clearings, because an aged tree has fallen, or where there is dense undergrowth.

Again as in conifers, there are few real woodland specialists, although some birds may seem for at least part of the year to be very closely associated with a particular tree. An excellent example of this is the Jay. Of the crow family proper, all of which are tree-nesters, it is the Jay that is perhaps the most typical and constant denizen of deciduous woodland, its harsh calls and bold white rump both well suited for contact and communication in the conditions of poor visibility that prevail in the undergrowth and up in the trees. As omnivores, Jays will take whatever food is available, in summer mixing worms and other soil animals from the leaf litter of the woodland floor with the eggs, nestlings and fledglings of other woodland birds. In autumn and winter, the diet becomes more specifically associated with woodland, as tree fruits (especially large tough seeds like acorns) feature prominently. Ecologically, the Jay is often regarded as a major factor in the perpetuation and spread of oak woodland, because of its habit of picking acorns from the canopy and flying off some distance to bury them in soil as a food cache against extremes of winter climate. In flight, with acorn in its beak, the Jay looks top-heavy, and its characteristically sporadic wingbeats seem even less likely than usual to keep it aloft until its mission is completed! Many of the hidden acorns are not retrieved by the Jays, and some subsequently germinate to produce new woodland.

Superficially, it would seem that deciduous woodland should offer excellent feeding to the seedeating finches, but the wood itself is not particularly rich in small seeds, save where penetrated by clearances in which a grassy or herbaceous understorey can develop. This helps to explain the relatively small number of this large group of birds found in woodland proper. Although as their colloquial name suggests they rely heavily on seeds of various sizes to provide the bulk of their diet, most seedeaters will take occasional flowers and fruitlets, and certainly unripe seeds from early-flowering plants such as dandelion, which become available in spring when last season's seed stocks are at their lowest ebb.

In the breeding season, most finches feed their young (at least in the early stages of growth) on a protein-rich collection of various small insects. Perhaps to take best advantage of the high insect populations on the flush of leaf growth, most seedeaters are mid-summer breeders. This allows them to build nests when trees are in leaf, providing maximum shelter.

Nevertheless, within the group of finches found in the broad-leaved woods of Britain and Ireland is to be found as good an ecological gradation of beak size and shape in relation to feeding as anywhere else in the world of birds. This gradation, coupled with a range of feeding sites extending from the woodland floor to the canopy, offers the main clues as to how these seedeaters partition their food resources.

All have the basic triangular (or better pyramidal) beak, and rounded skulls with relatively strong muscles powering the jaw action for seed crushing. Smallest of the group, and with the smallest beak, is the Redpoll, feeding mostly on the ground and on the seeds of small herbaceous plants and grasses. Slightly larger and more pointed is the beak of the Chaffinch, again feeding predominantly on the ground but on larger seeds. Next in the size scale comes the Greenfinch, with an altogether stouter beak, wider and deeper in relation to its length, for crushing larger seeds on the plant or on the ground. At the top of the scale are the heavy-headed, massive-beaked Hawfinches, capable of crushing the stones of tree fruits like wild cherry and damson to extract the nutritious kernel within. Some are said to exert incredible pressures in excess of 200 lb per sq in (36 kg per cm^2)! The inside of the beak has strongly ridged grooves to hold the stones in a vice-like grip. Hawfinches spend much of their time in the canopy, descending to feed on fallen stones late in the winter.

Not surprisingly, with a beak of such power, Hawfinches are also well able to deal with tree seeds like beech mast, or the toughest of all, hornbeam. The major concentrations of Hawfinches in Britain are in central and south-east England, and may possibly be associated with the distribution of the hornbeam as a favourite food. Certainly woods with plenty of beech and hornbeam are well worth searching for this elusive bird. Although the biggest of our finches and with bold white wingbars, Hawfinches are very shy, and by far the best way to locate them is to wait, watch and *listen* quietly for their Robin- or Song Thrush-like 'tchick' call, which is rather more abrupt and clicking than either of these well-known species.

Rather more specialised is the Goldfinch, which has tweezer-like elongated mandibles for extracting seeds from the spine-protected seed heads of thistles and teazel. Another specialist is the Bullfinch, with a beak more rounded in profile than the others. The peg-like tongue resembles that of the parrots, and beak and tongue combine to rotate flower buds, removing the outer scales so that the nutritious flower initial within can be eaten. For the Bullfinch, buds are a major food source during the late winter, helping to avoid excessive feeding pressures on a steadily diminishing seed crop under pressure from the other seedeaters. As the Woodpeckers are amongst the most arboreal of birds, it is hardly surprising to find the two Spotted Woodpeckers, Great and Lesser, firmly attached to the woodland habitat. Broadly speaking, they are adapted to live on insects and their larvae. Often this food source is concealed deep in crevices or beneath sheets of bark, or it may be that the larvae are tunnelling within the actual timber, and these are the sites that the Woodpeckers alone are able to exploit successfully.

The normal Woodpecker beak is relatively long, but very robust, and tapers to a chisel-edge rather than to a point. The skull is heavy and strong, and in some cases shock-absorbing tissue is located between the bones supporting the beak and the rest of the skull. This woodworking apparatus is powered by strong neck muscles, and functions much as a hammer-and-chisel, with the

55

'blade' end inserted by a hammering blow of the head, and then twisted to remove a flake of wood from the side of the excavation. In this way concealed food can be reached, and the length of beak and power of muscles determines the types of timber and depths to which any particular Woodpecker can probe.

Obviously such mechanical power is also well suited to opening the seeds and nuts of forest trees — hornbeam, beech, hazel and oak in particular — that most other birds find too large or too tough to handle. In this case, the nut is often lodged in a favourite crevice in the bark, which serves as a 'vice' while the nut is prised open and the nutritious kernel extracted. Similarly, when it comes to the breeding season, Woodpeckers excavate flask-shaped nests in tree trunks; these constitute a safe site, rarely exploited by other birds and then only usually by species occupying at 'second hand' old Woodpecker nests.

Beside their beaks, the Woodpeckers are supremely well adapted to their habitat in possessing powerful feet, with strong claws (arranged, unusually for most birds, two pointing forward and two backward) to give good grip on the bark, however smooth. Their central tail feathers are specially strengthened and inflexible, and serve as an additional prop, a shooting-stick almost, to support the woodpecker as it hammers, so they always operate head uppermost. Great and Lesser Spotted Woodpeckers have tongues that are exceptionally long, often protrusible for some inches, with a hardened and barbed tip, which is used like a harpoon to extract larvae from their tunnels.

'Drumming', by hammering on a suitably resonant branch, is a characteristic of both the Spotted Woodpeckers. This far-carrying sound is used to define territorial boundaries, and together with their short penetrating calls is well suited for forest communication. Surprisingly, in these technologically enlightened days, argument still raged as recently as the 1980s as to whether the drumming noise was produced mechanically or vocally, with many eminent and apparently expert naturalists assuring their fellows that the beak tip was always held clear of the branch during its production. Once a microphone small enough for the job had been designed, a few neat experiments with the microphone embedded in favourite drumming branches soon proved that the noise was produced by hammering of beak on branch. Doubtless the 'shock-absorbing' tissue pad between beak and skull helps prevent Woodpeckers from continuous headaches!

The last of the deciduous woodland 'specialists' is perhaps the least expected. The Woodcock is so unlike the rest of the wader family in habits and habitat that it holds a special fascination for many birdwatchers. For a start, its preferred habitat is woodland, winter and summer alike, not the marshes of the mudflats. Most favoured are woods with a deep layer of leaf litter, with some areas of dry ground suitable for nesting and some expanses of damp soil for feeding. These wet areas, rich in the worms which are the major item in the Woodcock's diet, are usually kept perpetually moist by seepage from underground springs. Beside this mixture of wet and dry ground, Woodcocks also require open glades for their display flights.

Both in winter and in the breeding season, the Woodcock is widespread in Britain and Ireland, more so than most birdwatchers would imagine as its secretive habits often keep it from view. In southern England it is a bird of oak woods, in the north of Scotland a bird of birch scrub — so catholic are its tastes.

Woodcock

Although because of its excellent camouflage the Woodcock may be difficult to spot, once seen it is very distinctive, with a delicately streaked and mottled rich brown plumage, absolutely ideal for camouflage against a background of dead leaves or bracken. Most often, whether on the nest or feeding, the Woodcock will rely on this amazingly good camouflage and crouch down, unmoving, until you are within a few feet (or even inches)! It has a disproportionately large beak, about 3 in (7.4 cm) long, and probes in the soft soil for earthworms and insect larvae like leatherjackets. The rather swollen tip to the beak contains numerous sensitive nerve endings which allow the Woodcock to identify its prey. Feeding at such a depth would seem to present difficulties if a mouthful of mud is to be avoided with each worm. The Woodcock manages this by means of a special skull adaptation. The nasal bones (which support the upper part of the beak) are long and flexible, and not rigidly attached to the roof of the skull between the eyes. Special muscles can pull the nasal bones back, allowing just the tip of the beak to open and the worm to be grasped and eaten.

The Woodcock is a crepuscular bird, feeding and flying in the poor light of late evening, and so has evolved large eyes for better night vision. These large eyes make the head seem large and angular, and as it flies off between the trees the Woodcock is so plump-bodied and round-winged that it could almost be mistaken for an owl.

Although making generalisations is inevitably dangerous where birds are concerned, because of the high mobility that flight allows them and because of their opportunist outlook so far as diet is concerned, there is merit in looking at the birds of deciduous woodland on the basis of three broad habitat categories.

The first of these is coppice. Coppicing entails clear-felling a whole tract of woodland at regular intervals of between 15 and 40 years. Thus few trees have substantial trunks, instead forming 'stools' from which a number of straight, slender and erect stems rise. Stools are rarely more than a few feet apart, and the slender trunks rise to form a canopy with few perforations. Because of their closeness, side branches are few and poorly developed. The surface area of the almost-flat canopy (viewed from above) is obviously less than when large trees billow (almost like cumulus clouds) through it, reducing feeding areas. With a continuous canopy, too, the ground vegetation is sparse and the shrub layer bushes such as elder are few and far between.

The second category contains so-called 'standards' — mature, typical trees but relatively closely spaced, so that as in the coppice the canopy is complete. However, viewed from above it has a much more irregular appearance, as adjacent trees have canopies that are dome-shaped rather than flat, increasing the surface area (and thus the food-carrying capacity) very considerably. As the canopy only becomes complete when the trees are full-grown, the supporting branches are both more numerous and much more robust than in coppice. Major trunks are many yards apart, but once the canopy nears completion overhead sufficient light is excluded to limit the undergrowth to a few spindly elder bushes and the occasional patch of bluebells or dog's mercury.

The third and last category can best be called 'gladed'. Here most of the trees will be majestically isolated or in groups of two or three. The patchwork of open areas between them will be filled with various shrubs, herbaceous plants and grasses, and it is easy to imagine the great increase in both feeding and nesting sites that tempts so many more individuals of more species to woodland of this type, which provides the best birdwatching of all.

What sorts of birds are to be expected in these three deciduous woodland habitat types? In coppice, because of the lack of branches and poor development of undergrowth, numbers both of species and of individuals breeding within such areas are poor. The winter picture is little better, as, although Tit flocks will search the bark, the rather uniform leaf litter apparently contains less in the way of small invertebrate animals to interest the various members of the Thrush family than other woodland types, and the whole structure of coppice does not offer adequate shelter for overnight roosts to develop.

The scanty and ephemeral nature of the ground vegetation, and the scarcity of ivy, greatly restrict the nesting possibilities for the 'generalists' — adaptable birds like the wren, robin and blackbird — but there is usually a reasonably high proportion of decaying timber. This provides good feeding and abundant nesting opportunities for the two Spotted Woodpeckers, and also the diminutive Treecreeper. Treecreepers feed mostly on small insects, spiders and the eggs and larvae, and on other small animals that tend to abound sheltering in cracks in or behind decaying bark. Their long, slender and very finely-pointed downcurved beaks must be ideal for extracting such tiny items from the crevices in which they are hidden. Their classical nest site, too, is in the slender cavity behind a flap of peeling bark on a dead or dying tree. Equally characteristic is the presence of two entrances (or perhaps one entrance plus an emergency exit) close to the boat-shaped nest.

Small, brown and fluffy in appearance, furtive and jerky in habits: that sums up the Treecreeper. Seen climbing a tree trunk, Treecreepers look almost like slender mice, but seen in flight, which is deeply undulating and rather feeble, they appear much dumpier and almost moth-like, so rounded are their wings. Their long tail closely resembles that of the Woodpeckers, with the shafts of the central feathers specially strengthened. As in the Woodpeckers (to which the Treecreeper is not related), the tail is used as a prop, the bird always moving head-uppermost on the trunk. This is a case of parallel evolution, where two unrelated birds have arrived at the same anatomical solution to their problems via the processes of evolution. Interestingly, not only are the tails structurally similar, but both birds have also evolved an unusual pattern of tail moult. The strong central pair are shed and replaced as one phase of the moult, while the remaining tail feathers do duty as a prop. Subsequently, the others are all shed together after the new strong central pair have grown to full length. This contrasts with almost all other birds where the tail feathers are shed and replaced in sequence, one pair at a time.

Treecreepers are most vocal, and often most easily seen, in late winter and early spring, when there are few leaves on the trees to interfere with the view. The song is much as would be expected from a tiny bird, high-pitched and silvery in tone, a descending trill with a last flourish of three clear notes, produced with rather unexpected volume. It is at this time of year that Treecreepers are displaying, a novel performance amongst birds and fascinating to watch as the birds chase each other in spirals up tree trunk after tree trunk, calling shrilly and excitedly all the while.

Where lesser branches have tried, and failed, to make it to maturity from the bole of the tree, small rot-holes commonly develop. These, and the slender decaying (and thus soft) trunks provide nesting habitat for two of the most difficult to distinguish of woodland birds. So great is the similarity between the Marsh Tit and the Willow Tit that it was only late in the nineteenth century that the Willow Tit was recognised as distinct from Marsh and added to the list of British birds. Subsequent investigations of stuffed birds in old museum collections revealed that the Willow Tit was not a newcomer to our shores; it had just not been properly recognised before. Even now we know far more about them, and are far more skilled in field identification, the two still present one of the greatest challenges to British birdwatchers. They are our only truly 'black capped' tits, the rest of the plumage being a subtle mixture of beiges and browns, toning delicately in a manner that would be the envy of autumn dress collections from famous fashion houses.

Not surprisingly, plumage differences between the two are small, and some individuals may not be identifiable, with certainty, unless they call. Unusually, it is possible to transliterate their calls meaningfully. Although both have a variety of sharp contact notes, only the Marsh Tit produces a rather explosive 'pit-chu', and only the Willow Tit a scraping 'dee dee dee' or 'chay chay' reminiscent of a squeaking gate hinge.

Both birds are common across England, the Willow Tit ranging further to the north and widespread in lowland Scotland, whereas the Marsh Tit only just reaches the Borders. Strangely, although both are widespread in Wales, neither occurs in Ireland, despite attempts to introduce the Willow Tit artificially.

The Marsh Tit is rather inappropriately named, as it is the Willow Tit that shows some preference for wetter woodland areas. Dense deciduous woodland is their preferred habitat, generally with trees like oak, hornbeam, hazel and beech that produce a prolific and nutritious seed crop that forms a valuable part of their winter diet.

Marsh Tits choose a natural hole or crevice, usually in a tree where a branch has broken off, but occasionally in a bank or wall, in which to build a nest. Sometimes they may take over a 'second-hand' nest hole of another species, and chip away the wood to modify the entrance, but only very rarely will they excavate their own nest in rotten timber.

The Willow Tit is perhaps more aptly named, as the soft-timbered willow is one of its favourite nesting trees. Willow Tits often breed in damp woodland, usually with many moss-covered old stumps. The essential requirement in the breeding area is a supply of such stumps, which must be softwood, alive, dying or decaying. Birch and elder are commonly used as well as willow.

In these stumps, the Willow Tit pair *excavate* their nest: a striking difference not just from Marsh Tits but also from other members of the Tit family except the Crested Tit of conifer forests. Although on sight it is often impossible to separate male from female in both Willow and Marsh Tits (she may be very slightly smaller) studies of colour-ringed Willow Tits have shown that the female does most of the work. Unlike Woodpeckers, which leave a conspicuous pile of droppings on the ground below their nest hole, the Willow Tits usually carry their debris 10 or 15 yards (metres) away, and for good measure may pulverise them too, leaving no tell-tale traces at the nest.

This excavating activity naturally demands strong and bulky neck muscles if the beak is to be effectively used as a combined hammer and chisel. These muscles, in turn, give the Willow Tit a distinctly bull-necked appearance, which, after some experience, can be one of the best ways of separating Willow Tits from Marsh Tits in the field.

Generally speaking there are increases both in species richness and in the numbers of individual birds to be seen in areas of 'standard' woodland compared with coppice. The proportion of decaying timber is probably little different from coppice, but the size of the branches which fall or split makes for considerably larger cavities, which are exploited by birds like the Stock Dove and Little Owl. The greater number and better structure of branches beneath the expanded standards canopy provides nest sites for large birds like the Wood-pigeon and Carrion Crow, and in some scarce but special woods allows the largest British regularly tree-nesting species, the Heron, to build heronries in which individual nests may be 4 ft (1.2 m) across and almost 1 ft (30 cm) deep, with Jackdaws and Tree Sparrows as 'signallers' nesting in the 'basement' of the bulky twig foundations. Here too will be found Mistle Thrushes, the largest of the Thrush family in Britain and Ireland. Warm days after the New Year will see all the local males high in the treetops proclaiming territorial boundaries, and the Mistle Thrush habit of continuing to sing in the teeth of the roughest of early spring gales has earned it the nickname 'storm cock'.

Mistle thrushes nest very early, often in March. The nest is a large, untidy construction in the fork of a major tree branch, built of grass and just about anything else that is handy; Mistle Thrushes were among the first birds to exploit waste polythene sheet as a nesting material! Such nests are obviously very conspicuous, especially early in the season, and Mistle Thrushes rely on aggression to compensate for this. Magpies, Jays and Crows, although larger than the Mistle Thrush, are everyday targets, and even a Buzzard will be treated to their wrath if it comes too near the nest. Marauding weasels, stoats and foxes are vigorously, and noisily, dive-bombed, and Mistle Thrushes are usually among the first to raise the woodland alarm when a roosting owl is discovered. Although the attack is not often pressed home as far as physical contact, the fuss is usually sufficient to distract the intruder or drive it away.

As their name suggests, Mistle Thrushes are particularly partial to mistletoe berries. Aristotle was aware of this liking, and his name for them — *viscivorus* — is derived from the scientific name for the mistletoe (*Viscum*) and means 'mistletoe-eater'. His epithet is retained in the scientific name for the Mistle Thrush itself, *Turdus viscivorus*. Although basically woodland birds, they feed much further out in open fields in summer than do Song Thrushes and Blackbirds, which may help them to subsist in rather poorer quality woodland.

Most insectivorous birds would be expected to benefit from the considerably increased canopy surface (thus supporting far more aphids, caterpillars and the like) of 'standard' woodland, but for many of them the absence of well-developed undergrowth probably imposes limitations because of the lack of suitable nesting sites. Hole-nesters like the tits (Great Tit and Blue Tit in particular, with their heavy dependence on massive numbers of winter moth caterpillars on oak on which to raise their young) can obviously flourish beneath standards, and the Blackcap and Chiff-chaff are two of the Warblers well adapted to exploiting such conditions.

Two exceptions (both rare) apart, the Warblers are all migrants, arriving from winter quarters in or near the Tropics to exploit the summer flush of insects, and later of fruit, in Temperate Region habitats. On the basis of their slender beaks, all would be classed as insectivorous; but especially towards the end of summer, when 'fuel' (in the form of stored body fat) is needed for the southward migration, all will turn to the sugar-rich, easily processed berry crop, with little indication of any difficulty in making this violent change in diet. The Blackcap and Chiff-chaff both form half of a pair of closely allied species.

Chiff-chaff and Willow Warbler, for example, are visually often inseparable, but have vastly different songs. Ecological separation of such pairs is often subtle, perhaps reinforcing the idea of the richness of this woodland habitat. Both these 'leaf warblers' are canopy feeders, picking insects off the undersides of leaves. Chiff-chaffs prefer taller timber, Willow Warblers scrub or undergrowth, but these differences are hard to detect where both are common, as in southern England. In consequence, Willow Warblers tend to favour gladed areas, and penetrate much further north into birch and willow scrub areas where the climate prohibits the growth of tall trees, whereas the Chiff-chaff manages perfectly well in areas of standards.

If Willow Warbler and Chiff-chaff are alike in plumage but vastly different in song, then the Blackcap/Garden Warbler pair are the reverse. The Garden Warbler is shades of nondescript greenish buff, whereas the Blackcap has a striking patch, black in the male, chestnut in the female and young. The seasoned ear, in practice, will often find little difficulty in separating the songs of the two, but there will be numerous occasions when a sight of the singer would help greatly. Both are well worthy of the name 'warbler' (unlike the Chiff-chaff!) and it is the Garden Warbler which is held by most birdwatchers to be the more melodious.

Blackcaps prefer the tall standard trees of mature deciduous woods because they choose song posts high up in the canopy, whereas the Garden Warbler is far more a songster in dense undergrowth or scrub, thus favouring gladed woodland. In spring, the Blackcap song is largely territorial in function, designed partly to attract a mate and partly to advertise the boundaries of that particular bird's territory. Later in the summer, and perhaps also when recently-fledged young birds are trying out their voices, a stealthy approach may achieve views of a Blackcap singing, it appears, quietly to itself. Such song seems to be produced slightly *sotto voce* or almost under the breath, and the bird producing it seems totally relaxed and oblivious. Quite what the function of this 'sub-song' is has not accurately been determined. It may genuinely reflect a time of relaxation when the pressures of the breeding season are receding. In many species, mimicry of other kinds of birds plays a part in the structure of the song: the Blackcap certainly does this, and it may well be that 'sub-song' is a time of singing practice and experimentation for younger birds, eager to impress in full song next summer.

In the gladed areas, increases in the numbers of birds to be seen are usually most apparent among the thrushes, warblers and finches, and there may well be twice as many birds, or more, as in a comparable area of standards. Such increases are probably attributable in the main to two features: the greatly increased structural diversity of the habitat in a physical sense, and the increase in both animal and vegetable food materials consequent on an increased diversity of plant species. Additionally, as there was an increase of vegetational surface area from coppice to standards, so there is an even greater one when glades are introduced amongst standard trees. Thus here is found the maximum nest site and food availability within deciduous woodland, an indication of the benefits of both the 'edge-effect' and of 'scrub' (in the form here of undergrowth) to bird populations. It is worth noting that the actual canopy area of mature trees is perhaps smaller than in a comparable area of standards. The effects of such a reduction, not so much in actual foliage but more in the insect life it supports, are difficult to assess. In the case of oak woodland, it should influence only those species dependent in a major way on oak (for example Great and Blue Tits feeding on winter moth caterpillars), because other birds are mobile enough and generally catholic enough in the food preferences to have easy recourse to adequate substitute supplies nearby.

Not unnaturally, the winter situation is similar, and again numerically it is apparent that the thrushes and finches derive most benefit from habitat of this

63

gladed nature. A variety of raptors and owls has appeared, able both to hunt mammals, insects and birds in the open glades and to prey on the increased numbers and variety of *all* animals, not just birds, available in this situation.

One of the raptors, the Sparrowhawk, is best seen in this habitat. The round-winged hawks (as distinct from the long-winged falcons) are adept at lying in wait, perched, for likely quarry, then pursuing it in a short hectic chase before striking it in flight with powerful talons set on long legs. Naturally the intended prey dashes for cover, and here the manoeuvreability conferred by the short broad wings allows the Sparrowhawk to follow every twist and turn through the bushes, where a Kestrel would either get tangled amongst the branches or just not be able to keep up. Sparrowhawks are most numerous in the woodlands of the west and north, having made a welcome come-back in numbers from very low levels in the 1960s caused by pesticide contamination. Recovery has been slowest in the east and southeast of England, but even here the indications of an increase are heartening.

Sparrowhawk

The male Sparrowhawk (as in the vast majority of the birds of prey) is conspicuously smaller than his female. She may be almost one third longer, and almost twice his weight. Naturally this size discrepancy influences the prey birds that they catch: Chaffinches and Tits, and perhaps occasionally something as large as a Song Thrush, are his limits, whereas she regularly takes various Thrushes and can handle birds as large as Woodpigeons. During the breeding

The glutinous ooze of estuarine mudflats teems with minute plant and animal life, rich feeding for often tens of thousands of waders, ducks, geese and gulls. Especially during the winter months, and spring and autumn migration, our estuaries may be vital to the survival of European populations of these birds.

A broad, slow-moving waterway typical of lowland Britain, a haunt of moorhen, coot, dabchick and kingfisher. Man has played a part in shaping many of these, despite their 'natural' appearance, and this was once a defensive military canal. Lush vegetation provides food, shelter and nest sites, and the adjacent ash wood holds a heronry with conveniently close fishing!

Gravel pits, and other flooded sites of mineral extraction, go some way towards compensating for wetlands 'lost' to agricultural drainage. They are particularly favoured by ducks and grebes in winter, and have the advantage that they can be 'shaped' during excavation to provide (as here) nesting islets for gulls and terns, and sandbanks suitable for waders.

Small lochans or tarns usually house a few moorhen, coot, mallard and dabchick, and some will provide breeding sites for less-common ducks such as wigeon, pintail and especially the tiny teal. In the remote highlands, waters such as this (or smaller) will be adequate for red-throated divers, and for the very rare few pairs of breeding black-necked grebes.

'Typical' English farmland, a mixture of fields with a wide variety of crops and stock, spinneys, larger woodland areas and a network of hedges. The woods and spinneys form reservoirs from which birds (and other animals of all sorts and sizes) move out to populate the whole countryside, emphasizing the value of the hedgerows as highways and breeding places.

Romney Marsh, in Kent, initially created by Roman engineers about 2000 years ago. In the summer, this close-cropped grazing marsh is home to lapwing, skylarks and yellow wagtails, while in winter it provides food for large flocks of ducks, geese, wild swans and waders (especially golden plover), particularly around shallow flooded areas.

Technological advances in farming have been just as rapid as in other industries, with equally dramatic results. Here an area of scrub has been cleared to reduce crop damage by rabbits and bullfinches, and the land surface is being re-shaped to allow arable farming machinery to work without difficulty.

Deciduous woodland of this type is amongst the richest of bird habitats. The major tree species here are oak and elm, both good sources of food and shelter, but at least as important is the physical structure. Uneven spacing increases the canopy area, wide glades lengthen the woodland margin (preferred by many birds for nesting and feeding), and within the glades herbaceous plants add further variety to the available foods.

When mature, the close-packed ranks of trees in commercially-managed conifer forests may seem sombre, but they still provide a home for many birds, including specialists like the crossbill and great rarities like the tiny firecrest. One major advantage is that parts are felled at regular intervals, providing a different habitat which for a few years encourages other birds such as tree pipits and nightjars.

Although some of the works of man may be beneficial to birds, there are areas where they are positively hazardous. This enigma occurs at Dungeness, in Kent, where the nuclear power stations provide nesting sites and good feeding for seabirds, while collisions with these power lines kill many birds flying after dusk, besides dramatically changing the visual aspects of the landscape.

Softly beautiful when clad in purple heather in late summer, the rounded outlines of the Cairngorms in Scotland provide a home for many of our mountain birds. In winter, their aspect is more severe when shrouded in snow, and conditions are so extreme that only specialist birds like the ptarmigan can survive.

MacGillycuddy's Reeks form a backcloth to a vast area of peat and bog in south-west Ireland. Areas such as this echo to the bubbling song of the curlew and the scolding cackle of the red grouse during the summer, but may be almost birdless during the winter months.

Promontories — this is Land's End, in Cornwall — are often good sites for watching seabird movements, as the birds pass close by their tips. Equally, they are important to migrant land birds as the first visible dry land to head for, to rest and feed after a long journey, so many bird observatories are situated in such places.

Puffins are gregarious birds, often gathering to bask sociably on a sun-warmed knoll in the colony. They are breeding birds of the cliff tops, either digging burrows in the springy turf or using the natural cavities in a rocky scree in which to lay their single egg.

The stacs of the Farne Islands, off the Northumberland coast, are spectacular seabird cities. The flat tops of the pillars are crammed with guillemots, as are the broader ledges of the cliff face, which may be shared with shags. In contrast, kittiwakes seem able to secure their nests to the slightest of protrusions, even under an overhang.

Extensive reedbed areas, specialised monoculture habitats of the common reed *Phragmites*, are beloved by bittern, marsh harrier, bearded tit and reed warbler. This is now one of the scarcest habitats in Britain and Ireland, but fortunately several of the best sites are protected as reserves like this, the Stodmarsh National Nature Reserve in Kent.

season, the female is very attentive to the young in the nest, and stays nearby on protective guard until they are fairly large. The male goes off and hunts during most of the daylight hours, returning (calling loudly) to leave food at regularly used 'plucking posts', where the female collects it and takes it to the nest. These plucking posts, surrounded by conspicuous quantities of feathers from the prey, are one of the best indications that Sparrowhawks are nearby. Her absence from the food hunting 'team' obviously puts the small male under considerable stress, but with typically neat evolutionary adaptation and timing the female has moulted all her flight feathers whilst incubating and during the early stages of raising the brood. Thus she is able to take on the role of major food provider, with her flight at maximum efficiency, just at the right time, and the larger prey that she provides helps the brood of young (sometimes as many as six or seven of them) to fledge satisfactorily.

Tradition would have it that the distribution of the Nightingale, the cowslip and the hop have much in common in England, and this is broadly true. Most Nightingales breed to the south of a line between the rivers Severn and Humber, preferring a well-developed and dense undergrowth, usually of brambles or nettles. Thus most Nightingales are found in woodland areas, usually of deciduous trees and very often of oak, with the mature trees widely spaced. Towards the north-western fringe of this breeding range, the wooded slopes of river valleys seem particularly to be favoured.

Over the last few centuries, the distribution of the Nightingale right across Europe has contracted considerably. Possibly this is in part due to wholesale trapping (particularly on the Continent) of birds for caging as songsters, or, even more unpleasant, for delicatessen eating. Though this regrettably still occurs, it seems more likely that the major factor in the decline is usually the loss of appropriate open deciduous woodland. This may be due to modern farming and its demands for full land usage and increased field sizes, or to modern forestry economics which all too often demand that broad-leaved woodlands should be replaced by dense plantations of conifers. Even within otherwise suitable deciduous woods, damaging management patterns may affect Nightingale numbers. Recent research has shown that even regular coppicing can provide suitable habitat (except in the first couple of years after clear-felling), but if coppicing ceases and the woodland matures to give an increasingly dense canopy, the exclusion of light prevents the growth of a good under-storey, and the Nightingales leave.

Generally, Nightingales are shy, inveterate skulkers, rarely venturing into the open, so this is a bird far more often seen than heard. Considerable patience, and quiet watching from semi-concealment in an area with several Nightingale pairs, a 'watch' in the old and attractive colloquial collective noun, and preferably with some paths to provide open ground, is required to obtain even fleeting glimpses. Sometimes, with good luck, a male may choose to sing from a perch in your line of sight, head thrown slightly back, throat bulging, to give the full audio-visual treatment. More often, apart from the song, much of what you will hear as you peer hopefully into the undergrowth will be the surprisingly varied repertoire of 'chacks' and 'churrs' with which the Nightingale scolds intruders from its place of concealment, or the soft 'wheet' call that the pair use to keep in contact. The voice of the Nightingale, heard solo at dead of night, comes through the clear, warm, early summer air as one of the most fabulous bird songs in the world. Regrettably, the song period is too short, generally only spanning the second half of May and through June, rarely reaching July. For quality, range and versatility the Nightingale never fails to impress, and for many its song is as near to perfection in British birds as we are likely to get.

Another characteristic bird of open, gladed woods is the Nuthatch. These occur most commonly in mature or aged woodland, especially favouring areas where the glades are substantial and grassy, and where beech, oak and sweet chestnut occur to provide winter food. Decrepit trees seem particularly attractive to them, but their distribution in England is erratic and often puzzling, as many apparently suitable areas have no Nuthatches. Because of their attractive grey and chestnut plumage, there have been attempts in the past to introduce Nuthatches to Scotland and Ireland (where they are totally absent), but these have not proved successful.

Although superficially similar to the Woodpeckers in habitat choice and in behaviour, the Nuthatch is generally considered to be more closely related to the Tits and Treecreepers. True, it climbs with great ease even on the trunk of the smoothest barked beech tree, but the Nuthatch's toes are arranged three forward, one back, as in the other families of birds within the passerine order, not two forward, two back, as in the woodpeckers. True, too, the Nuthatch has a disproportionately large, dagger-shaped beak just like a woodpecker's (another product of 'parallel evolution'), but the Nuthatch lacks the extremely long tongue that the Woodpeckers use to extract their food. Although they do take many insects and their larvae, particularly in summer, Nuthatches specialise in eating nuts. Larger and harder ones, such as chestnuts, beechmast and hazel nuts, are carried away in the beak to a suitable crevice in the bark and hammered open. This anvil treatment produces a characteristically intermittent noise which is one of the best ways of locating Nuthatches in winter.

There are other, subtler differences. Woodpeckers, with their specially strong tails, always move head-up on a trunk, but Nuthatches can move with similar ease head-up, head-down, or horizontally across a trunk, and close inspection through binoculars will reveal the reason. Their tails are short, and the tail feathers are of normal shape, flexibility and toughness and only rarely come into contact with the bark at all.

Nuthatches nest in natural cavities, usually in a decaying tree but occasionally in a deserted building. They take readily to nest-boxes, but other more extraordinary sites on record include disused woodpecker and sand martin holes, an old magpie nest and even some in Sussex haystacks! Neither the size of the cavity nor the entrance hole seems to influence the choice, and Nuthatches have a habit (unique amongst British birds) of cementing up the entrance (and in the case of the haystack nests the cavity walls also) with mud until the hole is of the right size. When using nest-boxes, they will also plaster round the lid, from the inside, making this difficult to remove without the risk of lumps of caked dry mud dropping onto the eggs and breaking them.

The nest itself is also of a unique type, so constant as to appear as an essential part of Nuthatch life. The eggs are laid on the floor of the cavity, on top of a layer of flakes of bark (especially yew or larch if this is available) or of oak or other leaves. There is no 'cup' as such, and when the incubating bird departs to feed or drink she covers the eggs with similar debris; so, on a superficial inspection, the occupied nest looks like the long-deserted winter lodging of a fieldmouse or dormouse.

The dual use of this well-structured gladed woodland in winter should not pass without mention. Besides the winter food, numerous and well-sheltered roosting sites are available in the lower vegetation layers, and recent research has indicated that for a bird like the blackbird the midwinter overnight weight loss (usually of body fat metabolised to keep the bird warm) can be reduced by up to 80 per cent by the choice of a prime sheltered roost site during bad weather. For many species these roosts may be used throughout the winter, but for others the period of peak use may be quite short (perhaps less than one month) and this, of course, does not detract at all from their usefulness; indeed they may be the more vital for such birds as an 'ultimate refuge' in times of severest stress.

Speaking of woodland in general, rather than of any particular type, there is a tendency among birdwatchers to rate 'quality' on the basis of the breeding birds present. Although breeding bird populations are probably more easily surveyed and assessed than winter flocks, the importance of woodlands in winter may often be underemphasised, using the same argument that midwinter, with long cold nights to survive and only short daylengths in which to gather food for survival, may be the most critical or dangerous time of the year for many birds. Such a situation is evidenced by the far more frequent squabbles that occur over shared food resources in winter.

Take the Thrush family as an example. Commonly, the woodland Thrushes are ground feeders, sifting through leaf litter or probing soft soil in the search for small invertebrate animals. In summer, and through autumn and winter, many spend a proportion of their time in the trees and bushes, exploiting the crop of soft fruit, and seeming to demolish it improvidently early in the light of the probable hard times to come. Only the Song Thrush has developed an exclusive food source, having mastered the techniques of extracting snails from their shells. Size of bird and size of beak go hand-in-hand, and broadly determine the birds' handling capabilities so far as the diet is concerned, be it fruit or small animals. When times become harsh, when perhaps snowfall has driven the Thrushes off the open fields into the woods to seek food in the as yet not snow-covered leaf litter protected by the trees, squabbles over food items both between species and between individuals of the same species become commonplace. Once again it is size that determines success in these squabbles, and commonly it is the smallest of them, the Redwing, that goes first to the wall, and the robust Blackbird and Mistle Thrush that survive the best, harrying other birds and driving them off any tit-bit they may discover.

The Tits, and a number of allied species such as Wrens, Goldcrests and Treecreepers, apply another approach, evidently with success. Outside the breeding season they tend to form flocks, dozens or sometimes hundreds of birds strong, composed of several species. This makes for the most effective feeding exploitation of the woodland, with birds exploring all vegetation layers from the ground up to the outermost twigs of the canopy. The many pairs of eyes within the flock are likely to spot particularly rich feeding areas quicker than a single bird, and those same pairs of eyes, always on the alert, will quickly and efficiently warn all present if danger threatens in the shape of a predator. In both these cases it is clear that contact and alarm calls communicate their information not just to the caller's own species but also to others in the flock. Otherwise, the general chattering of calls seems sufficient to keep the flock together.

These mixed flocks have a tendency to sweep through the wood in a rolling, swirling cloud of birds. Some birds will remain with the flock, continuously on the move over a wide area (Blue Tits and Great Tits for example). Others, such as Treecreepers, Marsh and Willow Tits, and Wrens, may only join the group activity as it passes through their winter home range.

Within the flocks, various species have evolved to exploit loosely-defined feeding zones, minimising competition when food resources become scarce. Broadly speaking, these are the ground, the trunk, branches and twigs. The Chaffinch and largest Tit, the Great Tit, with relatively long beaks, are often to be found at ground level, sifting the forest floor litter for food items. The Great Tit often extends its range to the tree trunks, there joining the Nuthatches and Treecreepers. The Wren, with a very similar beak to the Treecreeper, seeks the same types of food predominantly on the ground layer. Most of the Tits feed on the smaller branches and on the fine twigs of the canopy, augmenting insect food with plant material during the winter. Many have powerful feet which allow extreme agility, with birds often hanging upside-down while searching for food. The Blue Tit is an excellent example of a canopy feeder, as is the Longtailed Tit, which is perhaps the most anxious-sounding and vociferous of woodland birds, calling non-stop.

Counter to the general rule-of-thumb that most land bird distributions show a bias towards the south-east and proximity to Continental Europe are three deciduous woodland birds, widely distributed in the west but comparatively scarce or even absent in the east. These are the Wood Warbler, closely akin to the Willow Warbler and Chiff-chaff but distinguished by its shivering trill of a song and yellowish underparts contrasting with strikingly white underparts. The Wood Warbler is a bird of tall trees, shunning woods with a dense layer of ground vegetation and with well-developed bushy undergrowth. The Pied Flycatcher, with a tendency to polygamous pairing, is almost completely limited to the west of a line joining Exeter and Hull. It is typically a bird of damp sessile oakwoods, but in the north finds suitable conditions and adequate food among the lichen-encrusted birches and alders beside Highland streams and lochs.

Redstarts are forever active birds, restlessly flitting about amongst the twigs or down onto the ground to seize some insect or caterpillar, but their primarily insectivorous diet may be augmented in autumn by sugar-rich ripening berries. Their most distinctive feature, the orange-chestnut tail possessed by all ages and both sexes, gives rise to their name. The 'red' is obvious, but the 'start' is derived from the Anglo-Saxon word *steort* meaning tail. Although its original habitat in Britain may well have been sandy heathland with large pine trees, as is still the case in Scotland, the Redstart is now a bird of northern and western Britain, but rather strangely almost absent from Ireland. It seems in these parts to have adapted well to the loss of much of its ancestral habitat, and has become a bird of old deciduous woodland, particularly sessile oak, with slightly decrepit trees.

Redstarts are hole-nesters, and it is sometimes argued that sheer competition (from Tits, Pied Flycatchers, Nuthatches and the like) is the only restriction on the population in Britain. Overseas, though, Redstarts may face different problems. Ringing recoveries indicate that our Redstarts winter in West Africa, and a series of declines in the British population have been linked to periods of drought in the Redstart's winter quarters, in much the same way as the drought in the sahel region adversely affected the Whitethroat.

It would be wrong to close any discussion on woodland birds without making reference to the fact that many of them have shown sufficient adaptability to form the backbone of our garden bird population. Dunnock, Robin, Wren, Song Thrush, Blackbird, Blue and Great Tit and so on — the list is considerable, but perhaps not too surprising as it takes little imagination to visualise the gardens, particularly of country towns or of older suburbia and commuter regions, as extensions of a modified gladed woodland penetrating like green tentacles into truly urban areas. The Robin has endeared itself so much that it was voted our national bird some years ago, and rightly so as its popularity extends from the garden to the cards on the mantelpiece at Christmas. Equally, most householders appreciate the privilege of watching Tits hanging from garden-bird feeding devices, but despair at protecting the tops of their milk bottles from attack by Tits seeking cream. Even the tweed-plumaged Dunnock ('Dun' meaning brown and 'ock' meaning little), so shy and wary in Continental forests, are much at home in gardens, going about their business often in very close proximity but quite unflustered.

Two, perhaps less expected, examples will make the point more strongly. The Kestrel is the most widespread and numerous raptor in Britain, although in some western areas it may be locally outnumbered by the Sparrowhawk. It also seems to be the most adaptable, as Kestrels breed in a wide range of habitats: woodland, farmland, town parks and gardens, and even deep in the heart of a city. Their choice of nest site is similarly broad, including holes in trees, holes and ledges on cliffs and quarries, and buildings, even including the windowsills of high-rise flats! One of the seemingly few environmental benefits of our motorway network is that Kestrels have quickly adapted to hunting over the new territory opened up in broad grassy verges and embankments. Close observation of the Kestrel's hunting technique is well worthwhile watching through binoculars. Notice how the Kestrel hangs head into wind, wings beating rapidly on calm days, but with less movement in strong winds, hence the name 'windhover'. Despite the violent gyrations of body and tail to cope with changing winds, the head always remains rock-steady, eyes focusing downwards in search of prey. Kestrels will hover at a considerable height, and it is no surprise to see one at 100 feet (30 m) or more; all you can do is to marvel at the acuity of eyesight that allows prey as small as a beetle to be spotted at that range.

Once the prey is in its sights the Kestrel plummets down, braking sharply, wings outstretched at the last minute, before seizing the prey in powerful talons. Usually one of the sharp claws pierces a vital organ as the life is crushed out of the victim, but occasionally larger prey may be killed or decapitated in typical falcon fashion with a bite at the base of the skull. In many areas, voles and mice are the main prey, but these are often augmented by less glamorous snacks such as beetles and worms, and urban Kestrels prey largely on small birds.

We encounter Tawny Owls more often than the other members of their family, despite their nocturnal habits, partly because their quavering hooting is so obvious and so exciting, and partly because they have adapted so well to co-existence with man. Although primarily birds of mature woodland, they penetrate into the gardens of suburbia and, like the Kestrel, even into the heart of towns and cities such as London -- anywhere with parks and trees and a supply of mice and sparrows for food. Owls hunt on silent wings. Their feathers have a velvety surface and the leading edge of the wing has a comb-like fringe so that it does not swish through the air as the owl swoops with outstretched talons onto its prey. An alternative technique is to sit quietly in a tree, feathers blending in good camouflage with the trunk, and wait for the next meal to scamper along the ground below. The attack is then vertical, with wings held cupped like a parachute.

Tawny Owls start their breeding season early: hooting may start before Christmas, and often reaches a crescendo in February as the final squabbles over territorial boundaries are settled. The nest will be in a hollow tree or little-used building, and they seem able to gauge the availability of food in the coming summer (mostly small rodents and birds, but including worms and fish and frogs from garden ponds) with accuracy, and lay an appropriate number of eggs. None, or just one or two, if food is scarce, but up to ten if it is plentiful. The female starts incubating as soon as the first egg is laid, so (unlike most birds) the young hatch at intervals of roughly two days. In consequence there is a considerable disparity in size between the oldest and the youngest chick; and should the owls suddenly fall on hard times the largest will eat the smallest, then the next smallest . . . Although apparently bloodthirsty cannibalism, this behaviour does give the family the best chance of producing one or two healthy chicks, rather than having *all* the young perish from starvation. Unusually for birds, the young Tawnies will be dependent on their parents for two or three months while they learn to fend for themselves. Not until autumn do their parents start to object and chase them out of the home territory, so right through the summer months hungry 'ku-weks' will penetrate city, suburban and woodland nights as owlets let their parents know where they are.

The richness, variety and interest of woodland birdwatching, no matter where you are, should now be abundantly clear. Contrary to what seems to be common thinking, this is not just a summer feature but holds sway right through the year; indeed, as it may hold the key to their survival, winter woodland may, from a conservation viewpoint, often be rather more important than summer. An inevitable consequence of this is that the ways in which birds conserve energy and partition and exploit the available food resources in winter may be wholly as fascinating to the birdwatcher as are the many and varied strategies that they apply to maximise their breeding productivity during the summer months.

5 *Mountain and Moor*

The upland areas of Britain and Ireland are situated in the west and north as a result of the underlying geology of these islands. With all their remoteness and grandeur, it is easy to imagine that they have persisted almost since the dawn of time unamended and often even untouched by the works of man, but this is not always the case. The actual nature of many mountain top areas has not been shaped by man, but with increased leisure time and vastly improved travel facilities, these areas, once totally isolated, are now subject to frequent human presence year round by walkers, climbers, naturalists and winter sports enthusiasts. The ski-lifts provided for the last provide easy access to the high tops which previously would only be visited by those whose fitness, endurance and enthusiasm carried them up extremely arduous and sometimes dangerous mountain tracks.

At these altitudes — 3-4,000 feet (900-1,200 m) — exposure to the extremes of climate (rain, low temperatures, and strong winds in particular) affects not just visiting humans but also the plant life of the mountain tops themselves. Plant growth is often scanty (but often extremely beautiful in the case, for example, of the saxifrages) and always very slow. Thus damage, even minor, be it due to grazing by red deer or the introduced reindeer, or to the trampling of human feet or the passage of ski-lift construction vehicles, can take many years to restore, and in those years erosion may scour the scanty traces of soil, leaving bare rock upon which nothing will thrive, save perhaps a few lichens.

Considerable areas of moorland are regularly reshaped, particularly in Ireland, by the activities of local peat cutters seeking domestic fuel, and, more recently, by commercial concerns extracting vast tonnages of peat to amend the heavy or chalky soils of lowland gardens, hundreds of miles away. What is less often realised is the size of the moorland acreage — or better square mileage — that resulted from forest clearances. These clearances, mostly in the recent centuries, were carried out with the initial aim of increasing grazing land and replacing non-profitable (at that time) timber with more profitable stock. In upland areas, manmade impacts of this nature are exacerbated by the climatic conditions (primarily by heavy rainfall) and can easily be carried to extremes that parallel the creation of prairie farmland. Such a devastation has produced much of the moorland in Britain and Ireland, and in many cases it is easy to find the old pine stumps half-buried and semi-fossilised in the past. Thus, although, as with the conversion of lowland forests to farmland, it is possible to regard the initial limited clearances as beneficial to birds in general, the continual clearance has resulted in an impoverished bird population, with the Meadow Pipit predominating. In many ways, much as large moorland areas are essential to the ecological and habitat balance of our countryside, there is scope for reversion and many 'moorland deserts' can only be improved by sympathetic forest replanting programmes.

Meadow Pipit feeding a young Cuckoo

Relatively few small birds find the windblown and often wet expanses of moorland an acceptable home, but the Meadow Pipit is perhaps the most characteristic small bird of the mosses, heather, bracken, bog and rough grassland. Even for Meadow Pipits, much of moorland Britain is too bleak in winter and they descend to lower altitudes during the autumn, some migrating to southern Europe. For much of the year pipits seem to spend a lot of time on the ground, running about at high speed snapping up insects. They are small birds, rather like elongated Dunnocks with athletic legs, and, like the Dunnock, with plumage a tweedy mixture of dark streaks on a brownish or olive background, sometimes quite golden in autumn. This gives excellent camouflage against a peat or dry grass background. One exception to this earth-bound way of life is the display flight, when the male rises steeply 50 feet (15 m) or more into the air, then slowly descends — wings extended and fluttering rapidly, tail fanned — just like a parachute, producing all the while a cheerfully tinkling, trilling song.

Naturally, in this terrain the nest is on the ground, a deep grass-lined cup tucked away in the base of a tussock and very difficult to locate, so cautious are the birds. The female Cuckoo seems not to have this problem. Meadow Pipits are probably the commonest hosts of Cuckoos in Britain and Ireland, certainly in the uplands. In late May and June, female Cuckoos can be seen patrolling the moors, observing Meadow Pipit movements closely and thus locating their nests. As they move about, the Cuckoos cause great alarm, not surprisingly, and agitated Meadow Pipits follow them about, calling shrilly, sometimes attacking and even causing feathers to fly.

The Cuckoo is an amazing bird, its life-cycle an essay in the marvels of evolution. When the female returns from Africa, even if she is laying for the first time, she is able to seek out the correct habitat and host, so that the eggs she lays are close enough imitations in both size and colour to fool the foster parents. She hunts through her territory, locating appropriate foster nests, laying as soon as they are ready with a part complete or recently completed clutch. In Britain, most Cuckoos are associated with one of three common 'foster parents': Reed Warblers in marshland, Dunnocks on farmland, and Meadow Pipits on moorland.

Egg-laying takes but a moment in a swift visit. The Cuckoo's wings hardly stop beating as she lands on the nest, lays her egg, snatches up a host egg and departs. The Cuckoo egg is specially quick to develop, taking only 10 or 11 days and usually a couple of days faster than the host. The chick that emerges is muscular, and wriggling beneath its unfortunate foster brothers and sisters (or any remaining eggs), arches its back, braces itself with unusually well-developed embryo wings — and hoists them up and out over the side of the nest, where of course they perish.

Thereafter, the baby Cuckoo grows at a great pace, soon dwarfing both the nest and his foster parents, who must continually hunt for food to satisfy the incessant, but obviously very effective, wheedling cries for food. Even after it has left the nest (by which time the adult Cuckoos will all have departed for Africa) the fledgling produces a call that will stop *any* food-carrying bird in its tracks, and draw it (like a powerful magnet) to stuff its beakful into the tempting orange gape of the young Cuckoo. At least one unfortuate Wren is on record as having overdone it by falling into that capacious throat, suffocating both the Cuckoo and itself! Then comes the last episode in this amazing story: a month or more after the adults have migrated, the young Cuckoos set off, on their own, with nothing but their instinctive navigation systems to guide them, accurately, to their wintering areas in tropical Africa.

Curlew

With the absence of suitable song posts in the treeless moorland terrain, the use of song flights for display and for marking territorial boundaries seems logical for birds like the Meadow Pipit and the Skylark. Although both of these are pleasant songsters, however, it is the Curlew that is the most conspicuously noisy of moorland breeding birds, calling and bubbling all day — and often for much of the short midsummer night — over the heather and mosses of boggy areas. The other two species of wading birds breeding on our moorlands are much less conspicuous. The much smaller Dunlin has an attractive trilling song, but otherwise tends to be as inconspicuous as it can. The larger Golden Plover, though spectacularly handsome with its gold-flecked back and white-edged black breast, is rarely vocal and surprisingly secretive and well camouflaged considering its striking plumage. Although the Curlew will rarely be a target, the smaller birds take their lives in their hands during display flights, as they become conspicuous targets for the two moorland falcons, the Peregrine (which also inhabits the mountains proper) and the Merlin, which is smaller and would normally tackle prey not much larger than pipits. Clearly, though, in the course of evolution, the benefits of advertisement in this way to the population as a whole must have outweighed the hazard, as the technique is so widely used.

The Curlew's display must surely rank as one of *the* sights and especially sounds for the birdwatcher. The male jumps into the air and climbs steeply on rapidly beating wings. Once aloft, he hovers briefly before descending on stiff, vibrating wings, producing a continuous stream of the most thrilling calls, gurgling, bubblings and whistling, ending in the evocative 'coo-er-leew' from which its name is derived. The nest is always well concealed, often in a grassy tussock amongst the silver feathery plumes of bog cotton grass. For the sitting bird, the drab plumage is good camouflage, but it remains surprising that this rather gaunt, angular, gull-sized bird with disproportionately large beak can vanish so effectively when she shuffles down to incubate her eggs. Breeding Curlews are extremely wary. The male stands guard on a nearby hummock, sounding the alarm to call the female off her nest as soon as danger threatens. She sneaks away from the nest, long legs bent and head held close to the ground, but should the intruder continue towards the nest the pair will start a tremendous clamour of alarm calls. As a further distraction, the female may even land close to a marauding fox, and stumble along dragging one wing as if injured, in an attempt to invite pursuit of herself and to lure the predator away from the actual nest.

One other characteristic moorland bird deserves mention, not just as a specialist in year-round survival in this habitat, but because it has often in the past been considered to be the only bird exclusively restricted to Britain and Ireland. Expert opinion now supports the view, though, that the Red Grouse is only a distinct race of the Willow Grouse or Willow Ptarmigan, which is widespread in northern Europe and North America. Dark reddish-brown, seeming almost black at a distance, the cock Red Grouse occasionally stands on a hummock or boulder, and a closer view shows the white-feathered legs that often feature, silver mounted, in the Highlands as tourist-attracting brooches. Grouse tend to remain in concealment, crouched in the heather, until you almost step on them. Then they 'explode' in a heart-stopping flurry, whirring away on downcurved wings, cackling angrily.

Grouse are heavily dependent on heather shoots for food, with other moor-land plants such as crowberry and bilberry providing occasional alternatives. The number on any particular moor is partly determined by the nature of the soil; in limestone areas, numbers tend to be high, whereas they are lowest on thick peats overlying granite. They are game birds, and like others of their kind are shot for sport and because they are considered to be tasty to eat. In sporting circles, August 12th — the 'glorious twelfth' — is a red letter day as the first day of the shooting season, and for this reason, besides variations in their natural habitat, Grouse numbers are very much influenced by man. Lines of beaters, driving the birds over guns concealed in butts, used to be a province confined to the landed gentry, but now the ownership of a grouse moor has become a most effective land use, in financial terms, as the return from renting the shooting is far higher than from any agricultural use. Whatever one may think of shooting, this does coincidentally ensure the continued maintenance and survival of this type of moorland — a valuable service to the environment.

Grouse 'bags' have decreased markedly in recent years. It was thought initially that disease and particularly predation were responsible, which generated an intensification of the persecution by gamekeepers of birds of prey of all sizes, from Merlins to Golden Eagles. It is now known that predation affects only the non-breeding surplus of the population and does not affect the number of 'targets' available for the shooting season. What has also been clearly shown is that the major reason for the decline is a deterioration in the quality of moorland management and thus also in the heather quality. Heather moorland requires intensive keepering: drainage, fertilizer application and restrictions on grazing all have to be supervised. Above all, areas have to be burnt, in rotation, to ensure a continuous succession of young heather shoots for food, but the balance of new and old heather must also be carefully watched, as it is the older, deeper growth that provides shelter and nest sites.

As the moorland rises towards the mountains, penetrated by rocky buttresses and screes, and dissected by mountain streams, so it becomes the habitat of the Ring Ouzel, which is very much the 'mountain Blackbird' of the north and west, though strangely not numerous in vast tracts of apparently suitable high ground terrain in south-west England. Ring Ouzel territories are usually far larger than those of Blackbirds, presumably reflecting the difficulties of finding adequate food supplies in the harsher environment. Upland pairs usually choose stretches of land with occasional crags and isolated trees (often rowan or 'mountain ash') to serve as song posts for the male, and with sheltered gullies in which to build the nest. Only rarely will they colonise a stretch of moorland uniform in slope and nature and without some distinctive features.

In the far north, a few pairs may breed each year almost at sea level, nesting

77

on ledges on the cliffs, but most Ring Ouzel nests lie between 750 and 1750 feet (230-530 m) above sea level. The highest nest on record was at a staggering altitude of 3750 feet (1150 m) in the Cairngorms. The nest, made of coarse grasses, heather and a good deal of mud and lined with soft, fine dry grass, is often built in a crevice or on a rock ledge on a small crag or scree. Almost as common are nests in low vegetation, and some nests are built directly on the ground. One feature common to most Ring Ouzel nests is that they command a wide view of the surrounding countryside for the sitting bird to survey, and another is that they often have an overhang, usually close above, offering some protection from the often inclement weather. Occasionally birds will use crevices in old deserted barns or mine buildings as a substitute for crags, and there are several descriptions of nests actually below ground level in old mine shafts, the lowest 15 feet (405 m) down. In contrast, very few nests have been found more than 3 feet (1 m) above ground in trees. The nest is fiercely defended by both birds calling harshly and dive-bombing intruders, be they crows, stoats, foxes or even innocently straying humans or mountain sheep.

Although Ring Ouzels are often conspicuous in their open habitat, and emphasise this by choosing prominent singing perches, they are much wilder than their familiar lowland cousins. On the ground, they have the same jaunty approach as a Blackbird, scampering along, then pausing briefly to look and listen for food, flicking wings and tail and occasionally cocking the tail high, especially immediately after landing. The usual first clue to the presence of Ring Ouzels is a disjointed series of remote-sounding penetrating whistles, sometimes double-phrased. Despite its simplicity, it definitely has the character to fit well with the Ring Ouzel's wild habitat, and its very simplicity may add to its penetrating power or range in the boisterously windy weather prevalent at such altitudes. Their most characteristic call is a harsh, laughing 'tchack-tchack'.

As with Meadow Pipits, Ring Ouzels are migrants, mostly wintering in the Mediterranean basin. Because they are relatively short-haul migrants, they are amongst the earliest of our summer visitors to arrive back, many reaching the south coast early in March and the breeding grounds a few days later. Passage, including birds passing through Britain on the way to Scandinavia, may continue until early May. Return migrants begin to gather in flocks to meander southwards in late August and September, and a trickle of migrants often continues into November. The southward journey lacks the urgency of spring migration, and when numbers are swollen by the year's crop of young birds Ring Ouzels may occasionally be met with almost anywhere in lowland Britain favoured by migrant thrushes, the prime requisite being a plentiful supply of suitable berries including elder, hawthorn, rose and rowan. Again the harsh 'tchack' call and the conspicuously grey wings are useful recognition features.

Ring Ouzel

It is when the *real* uplands are reached, the high tops of north Wales and north-west Scotland, that the montane specialists proper are encountered. Western Ireland is omitted from this chapter as although fulfilling the altitudinal requirements and possessing its share of the excitingly rare botanical attributes of the mountain tops, because of its westerly remoteness from the main bulk of Europe it lacks many of the specialist birds. The Peregrine and the Raven are the exceptions to this generalisation. Over much of Britain and Ireland, the Raven is considered to be a bird of mountain and moorland or remote and unpopulated coasts, but this distribution is very much a manmade one, and not the Raven's habitat preference. Before intensive persecution by shepherds and gamekeepers during the nineteenth century, the Raven was

79

widespread even in the lowlands. Modern studies have shown that its evil reputation as a lamb-killer is largely unjustified. In hill country, lambing is hazardous, and weakly or still-born lambs commonplace. Almost always, it is these dead or dying lambs that are 'attacked', as the Raven is a scavenger, not a bird of prey. This scavenging habit, associated with sheep, is responsible for the Raven's extraordinary early breeding season. Apart from the carrion provided by sheep, hares or deer killed by severe wintry conditions, the major food for the young is the placenta (or afterbirth) from the hill sheep at lambing. Lambing is early in the hills, hence often in February, but almost always by March, the Ravens will have eggs. High in the mountains the female will regularly have to sit through blizzard conditions without budging, as even momentary exposure would kill the eggs. By June, the young will be well on the wing, but still moving around in family groups.

Like other large birds of mountain terrain, Ravens often have enormous territories. In remote areas, 10 square miles (25 km^2) or more may be needed to provide adequate food. Within this will be several nest sites, and a different one may be used each year. Some sites are ancestral, having been used for decades, sometimes centuries, by succeeding generations. In these cases the nest is really bulky, as each year more branches and fresh greenery are added to it. Some nests are in trees, but probably the majority are well-protected and inaccessible on rocky crags. In 'off' years such nests may be 'borrowed' by a pair of Peregrine Falcons. The Raven pair during the breeding season will be vociferously aggressive to neighbouring Kestrels, Peregrines or even Golden Eagles, but they seem to take special delight in mobbing Buzzards. Their broad finger-tipped wings and long, wedge-shaped tail give them good flight control, and they swoop and dive all round the intruder.

Buzzards are no mean fliers themselves, and can easily dodge the attacks; often it is difficult to dismiss the thought that the birds are all enjoying their mastery of the air and just playing. Much the same comment can be made about some Raven relatives: Choughs, for example, soaring in the updraughts of our cliff-girt western coastline (especially in Ireland), or, much more mundane, Rooks cavorting in the skies over their rookery. For the Raven, these aerobatic skills are brought out to the full during courtship display. The pair will roll and tumble in the air, occasionally locking their talons belly to belly and falling head-over-heels for hundreds of feet before pulling up in a feather-tearing turn. All of this is accompanied by the Raven's gruff honking croak — an unmistakable noise echoing hollowly off the surrounding crags.

If Raven territories are considered to be vast, then some Golden Eagle territories are truly enormous, sometimes approaching 40 square miles (100 km^2) in extent. As with the Ravens, the size is linked directly to the ease or otherwise with which food may be obtained, and within the territory there may be several nest sites, occasionally in trees, rather more often on crags. With a total population in Scotland (there are a couple of pairs also in northern England) of as little as around 300 pairs, and most of these in genuinely remote and difficult country, finding Golden Eagles is not the easiest of tasks for the birdwatcher, but it can be one of the most spectacularly rewarding. The birds themselves are powerfully majestic, with spectacular display flights, but a true measure of their power is to see one stoop at a mountain hare or a red deer calf

Golden Eagle

on the flanks of a hillside and to hear the rush of air past outstretched wings and talons. In the historical past, Golden Eagles were outnumbered both on the coast and inland by the White-tailed or Sea Eagle. Both species were persecuted as sheep farming increased, the Sea Eagle to extinction, although attempts to reintroduce them are at present under way in north-west Scotland. Sadly, the persecution of Golden Eagles continues, both by shepherds who (almost always wrongly) consider them to be lamb-killers, or by gamekeepers who object to the chaos caused during a Grouse shoot when an Eagle passes over the moor, during a drive, scattering birds in all directions. In the post-war years, Golden Eagles suffered seriously from the effects of persistent organo-chlorine pesticides used in sheep dips and accumulated through food chains at the top of which were the Eagles. Now this particular adverse pressure has been removed, but as an unfortunate consequence of our mobility and urge to explore remote places disturbance by climbers and hill walkers is the major threat to the breeding success of some Eagle pairs.

The Peregrine Falcon population also suffered severely from the ill-effects of persistent pesticides, but as for the Golden Eagle this particular threat has been lifted and the long-term effects of the poisons concerned are gradually working out of the ecological system. As a result, Peregrine numbers have risen hearteningly almost to pre-war numbers, despite continuing and pointless pressure from illicit egg-collectors. Whether Peregrines will be able to continue their reinstatement process under the most recent threat is less certain.

Peregrine Falcon

Falconry, in Britain and Ireland but especially in Continental Europe and the Middle East, has risen greatly in popularity, and the Peregrine, long considered the master hunter by falconers (and by ornithologists who have watched enthralled as a Peregrine 'stoops' in a power dive at potential prey) now commands an enormous price on the black market. Despite the conservation consequences, the illegality of the operation and the heavy fines that are now imposed for removing young Peregrines from the nest, the cash returns are so high that this has become the major threat to the British and Irish Peregrine population, just as it had become apparently the most secure of the various populations round the world.

One bird of the high tops, related to the Red Grouse, that does occasionally feature in the diet of the Golden Eagle is the Ptarmigan. Over much of its breeding range in the Highlands, the Ptarmigan is confined to the arctic-alpine heath vegetation zone above about 2,000 feet (600 m) altitude. Here bilberry and crowberry, mixed with heather, provide its main food year-round, because the Ptarmigan has evolved adaptations to living in this zone even during winter snows. In summer, it is mottled greys, browns and fawns, blending perfectly with the stunted, sparse vegetation and lichen-covered rocks. Camouflage is vital for a terrestrial bird, rarely flying far and thus vulnerable in the extreme to a hunting Eagle as it sweeps at speed round the shoulder of a hill. As winter

Ptarmigan

approaches, the Ptarmigan in its autumn moult gradually becomes whiter, until (save for its tail feathers) it is snow white and ideally set up for winter camouflage. This is not all, however: during the winter snows, the Ptarmigan happily forage amongst the vegetation, burrowing down and living beneath the snow covering, which provides good insulation in an apparently totally inhospitable environment. Ptarmigan feet are feathered to the tips of their toes, so should they venture out onto the snow heat loss is minimised by the insulation the feathers provide at this point of contact.

Perhaps because humans are still something of a novelty to them, and such humans as they meet on the high tops are not showing any obvious intent to persecute them, Ptarmigan and the two other high tops specialists, the Dotterel (a wader with the roles of the sexes reversed, as in the Red-necked Phalarope) and the Snow Bunting (which strangely has its white plumage in summer, becoming drab in autumn when it migrates south to various coastal marshes to spend the winter), are extremely approachable. This confiding nature allows such superb views of the birds that the arduous business of climbing up to their high-level habitat is forgotten.

Much the same can be said of all birdwatching in mountain or moorland

83

terrain — it is arduous. Not only this, but on occasion it can be dangerous: the weather changes with great speed in the hills, and the possibilities of an ankle injury, getting lost in fog or cloud or being overtaken by a blizzard should not be lightly dismissed. Sensible precautions are easy to take in the form of adequate food supplies, more than enough warm clothing, and footwear up to the task. A note of your intended route should be left when you set out, and it is worth carrying map and compass, and a whistle or a brightly coloured anorak, too, to help attract attention in case of accidents. On the mountains and the moors, birds may sometimes seem few and far between, but birdwatching in this habitat, though tough going, is usually well worthwhile.

6 Coasts and Islands

Just what is it that makes Britain and Ireland so spectacularly fascinating for seabird enthusiasts? What is it about them ecologically that is so special that (for example) about 70 per cent of the world population of Razorbills nest here? For the specialist seabirds, perhaps the answer lies largely in the nature of our rocky coasts and islands. Most good seabird sites are remote from human presence, and feature precipitous cliffs, guarded by treacherous and often rough seas. Thus they are natural reserves in themselves, with little need for fences or notices, so effective is this protection — even against birdwatchers wishing to count seabird colonies or simply seeking a better view.

Much of the western and northern coastline of Britain and Ireland is rocky, and much of it deeply indented by coves and bays. Offshore are myriad cliff-girt islands of all sizes, and this whole coastline enjoys access to the shallow seas of the Continental Shelf, for much of the year rich in fish of all sorts and sizes. This wealth of seabirds is very much a summer feature though. During the autumn and winter months these shallow inshore waters are often whipped into a frenzy by the prevailing south-westerly winds, and most of our seabirds find less trouble feeding either by migrating south or by moving to less broken seas well away from the coastline.

In the east and south, the coasts are generally low-lying, the seas murky and much disturbed by the shipping passing by or polluted by the concentrations of industrial development on many of our own estuaries and on the Continental coast of the North Sea and the Channel. Add to these the summer disturbance caused by expanding seaside resorts, holiday camps, camping and caravan sites and marinas, and it becomes easier to see why the seabirds of the east coast in summer are restricted almost to the gulls and terns in species, and to low numbers of those. From Yorkshire northwards the position improves as the coastline again becomes principally cliffs, but to the south, even where cliffs occur, they tend to be of friable chalk and unsuitable for many seabirds to nest.

Gigantic and magnificent as a spectacle as some of our cliffs and stacs are, rising 1000 feet (300 m) or more sheer from the sea, they can be devoid of birds. The rock must be of the right type with strata and fractures producing a terrain suitable for the wide variety of seabird nests. Caves, for example, provide sites for Black Guillemots and in some areas for Rock Doves and the spectacular Chough. This red-billed ant-eating member of the crow family has a particular delight in riding the fierce updraughts of air at the cliff face, manoeuvring and tumbling skilfully about on broad wings with conspicuously 'fingered' ends. The slots between the wing feathers that these 'fingers' produce play a considerable part in aerodynamic control. Smaller crevices in the cliff face provide safe sites for Razorbills and Puffins to lay their eggs. Boulder screes, which may form at the top or bottom of a cliff, or midway between, house more Razorbills and Puffins, with petrels and Manx Shearwaters, Cormorants and Shags, for good measure. The cliff ledges themselves need to be more or less horizontal to be of use: hence the importance of how the rock fractures. On Skokholm, off Pembrokeshire, for example, the old red sandstone strata have come to lie in a vertical plane with successive movements of the earth's crust. Erosion has removed the softer rock, leaving upstanding hard knife-edges set far too close for the comfort of nesting seabirds, whereas on nearby Skomer the rock is granite and the ledges horizontal, and seabirds abound. Ledge-nesting birds include several gull species, Guillemots, Kittiwakes and Fulmars.

The Puffin, perhaps more than any other seabird, has the ability to arouse the enthusiasm and fascination of mankind — not just the birdwatcher. Perhaps it is the upright, manikin-like stance, or the 'evening dress' plumage that causes this, or perhaps it is its busybody enthusiasm to observe and participate in all the social goings-on in the neighbourhood that endears the Puffin to us. Although an easy bird to *watch*, especially at colonies (like the Farne Islands) where it is used to human disturbance, for all its handsome charm and popularity, the Puffin is notoriously difficult to *study*. Despite the spectacle when a whole large colony decides to indulge in an evening flypast, the rest of its coming and goings are fickle in the extreme, and Puffins do not show the faithfulness to the same nest site year after year that is almost expected of seabirds and perhaps best exemplified by the Manx Shearwater, where pairs will return to breed in the same burrow for many years in succession. When they visited the huge puffinry on St Kilda, remotely situated 40 miles (65 km) west of the Outer Hebrides, the Victorian naturalists and pioneer bird photographers the Kearton brothers recorded this flypast as sufficient to darken the sky and necessitate increased exposure times. Being well-equipped, they had with them umbrellas which they put up, not (as you might expect) to protect themselves from droppings but from the showers of feather parasites dropping like rain from the wheeling masses of birds overhead!

The Puffin is a cavity nester, digging or choosing tunnels in boulder screes or cliff-top thrift and turf and evicting rabbits from their burrows if necessary. Where, as on St Kilda, there are no rabbits, the Puffins will excavate their own nests, their short strong legs with powerfully clawed feet doing a swift job. Deep down this burrow the single chick is raised, as drab in its sooty black down as its parents are elegantly colourful. Its beak, too, is vastly different from its parents'. The multicoloured red, yellow and blue parrot-like 'summer beak' of the adult Puffin is a temporary horny ornament, of use during court- ship and the breeding season. In winter it is replaced by a drab (but still functional) grey-black beak, a little shorter and much less deep in proportion. In the chick, the beak is of similar drab colour, but even smaller and more pointed, rather like a miniature Razorbill. Winter-plumage Puffins are not often easily or well seen, as most of our birds winter well out to sea. Usually only storm-driven birds give the opportunity to examine the sootier blacks and smokey whites that replace summer's elegance.

Over much of its North Atlantic range, the Puffin has decreased in numbers, sometimes drastically in recent years. In the south, this may not come as a surprise as the Puffin seems intolerant of disturbance, but in the north and west it is more serious. Here, some colonies have been estimated in the past as millions of birds strong, and obviously this area constituted a major stronghold for the species. *Operation Seafarer*, a census of all our seabird colonies mounted in 1969 by the Seabird Group, came up with a total of about half a million pairs, a grand total rather less than the individual totals for colonies visited by Ronald Lockley and James Fisher only 30 years before. No clear reason for the decline has been found, which is worrying. In Britain and Ireland we can take comfort from the fact that recent surveys indicate that the situation has apparently stabilised, but elsewhere in northern Europe reports indicate that declines and breeding failures continue, so the overall picture is not so hopeful.

That such a decline should occur in the middle of the conservation- enlightened twentieth century is the more remarkable when the past per- secution of the Puffin is taken into account. Up to the end of the nineteenth century, and sometimes beyond, remote island communities depended heavily on seabirds, and their eggs and young, as year-round staple items in their diet. Eggs were collected and laid down in ashes for later consumption, and adult and young birds were caught by fowlers using nets or nooses, either being eaten immediately or being dried or salted. Expertise in fowling was invaluable to the islanders' well-being, and the toll of birds taken was often enormous. On St Kilda, where the community never numbered more than a few hundred souls, even in Victorian times the annual catch just of Puffins often exceeded 100,000 birds. The birds' salvation lay in the fact that this slaughter was also a harvest, and was strictly regulated at levels that past experience had shown to be tolerable by the birds. Excessive killing could not be allowed because the same colonies had to be 'cropped' in succeeding years.

On numerous other islands, particlarly those close inshore where some form of farming activity was carried out, man has caused additional problems to seabird colonies by introducing brown rats. Lundy, the so-called 'Isle of Puffins' lost most of its Puffins in this way. There are other cases where the Puffins themselves have played a part, too. On Grassholm, now a famous gannetry of Pembrokeshire, it has been suggested that excessive burrowing by large numbers of Puffins led to rapid drying and fragmentation of the thin layer of topsoil, and that wind and water erosion soon reduced the island surface to its basic rock structure.

Razorbills

Most Razorbill colonies are relatively small, and often interspersed amongst those of other auks, especially Guillemots. Because the nest is hidden, observation and counting can be difficult, but on remote islands where human visitors are few, the confiding nature of the Razorbills, allowing extremely close approach without distress, more than compensates for this. The Razorbill is perhaps the most handsome of our seabirds: the plumage is an immaculate contrast of black and white. On the head, the black is offset by an elegant white trim on the beak and by a fine white line of tiny feathers (looking almost like fur) running from the beak to the eye. It has been suggested that these white marks may form some sort of sighting device helping the Razorbills to catch fish when hunting under water.

Structurally, the Razorbill and the other auks are part-way, in an evolutionary sense, to becoming the penguins of the northern hemisphere. They lead divided lives, partly spent in the air, partly spent on land, and partly on or under the water, but their major adaptations are to the last mode. The wings are reduced in size and stiffened (though not to the extreme degree seen in penguins) which results in rather poor flight characteristics but excellent underwater propulsion. The head and body are streamlined and the eyes deep-set, ideal for rapid underwater progress, with the extended webbed feet serving as do the control fins of a submarine. The body is purpose-built for deep diving, with an immensely strong rib cage. The ribs are fused, through projecting spurs, to each other and to a rigid backbone and breastbone, forming a robust box protecting the vital organs from the crushing pressure of the sea.

Operation Seafarer counts suggested that the Guillemot population exceeded the half-million mark in Britain and Ireland, and Guillemots seem to be holding their own in the modern environment despite the all-too-often-shown tragic pictures of birds coated in oil following an involvement with oil spillage. The fact that recent research indicates that Guillemot population levels as a whole can tolerate the deaths due to oil should in no way allow us to forget the suffering caused to enormous numbers of individual birds and the inhumanity behind the release of the oil, which is often due to human carelessness, or worse to the deliberate washing out of tanks at sea.

Just looking at the seabird stacs of the Farne Islands or St Kilda, or looking at photographs of similar colonies, confirms that Guillemots pack tightly onto stac tops or cliff ledges, standing upright and looking rather like several months' uncollected deliveries of milk bottles on a huge doorstep. Each new arrival, trying to find a space in which to land, causes noisy confusion as he blunders amongst his fellows. The Guillemot has one of the simplest of all nests, merely laying its single egg on the rock, with no nesting material, not even a few sprays of seaweed for decoration. The egg that allows such simplicity is a masterpiece of evolutionary design. It is large, 4 or 5 inches (10-15 cm) long, and tapered sharply rather like a pear or a child's top. If knocked accidentally, as so easily happens in such crowded colonies, it rolls in a tight circle but stays on the ledge. In similar circumstances, the normally-shaped Razorbill egg would have as much chance of survival as a breakfast egg rolling on the kitchen table — so Razorbills tend to be crevice nesters. Guillemot eggs are also conspicuously variable in ground colour (from cream, through the duck-egg blues and greens to pink) and in the nature of the spots and squiggles on their surface, all as an aid for the home-coming bird to recognise its own egg amongst many others.

Razorbills and Puffins bring fish to their young in beakfuls, often ten fish or more at a time and sometimes up to fifty or even beyond in the case of the Puffin. The Guillemot, in contrast, comes home with a single, much larger fish for its youngster. In the crowded circumstances of colony life, even feeding must be circumspect to avoid the unwanted attentions of a neighbouring greedy chick. The adult Guillemot extends its wings in an angelic posture, and brings them forward to form a screen round its chick. The fish is then transferred head-first, so that it can be quickly accepted and easily swallowed. When the chick is very young, not all the fish may get in at the first attempt, and replete Guillemot chicks can be a comic sight with several inches of fish tail dangling from the corners of their mouths. As a tribute to their digestive capacity, however, it is only a couple of hours later that the chick is clamouring for more.

Some Guillemots, particularly in the north, have a white eye-ring with a slender white line stretching back and closely resembling a pair of spectacles. Just what the function of this plumage variety (called the 'bridled' form) is, nobody knows. Nor is it understood why the proportion of bridled birds increases as you travel north. Guillemots from the more northerly colonies are of a different subspecies, too, and (unlike many subspecies) can be easily recognised from their milk-chocolate-coloured southern relatives by their almost black plumage.

The Black Guillemot is much less numerous than its larger relative, and is particularly a bird of the coasts and islands of the north-west. Jet black save for bold white wing patches, the Black Guillemot is a cave or cavity nester, usually in colonies of a few pairs. Its feet are bright vermilion, so bright as to be visible underwater even at long range. Unlike the rest of our auks, the Black Guillemot still lays two eggs (it is thought that laying just a single egg is an advanced evolutionary adaptation) and often manages to rear both young. Off-duty birds occasionally roost in buoys, emerging in a black-and-white cascade when their perch is rocked by the wake of a passing vessel. The solemn note of the bell-buoy is then joined by their improbable treble-pitched whistling tinkle of a call. Yet another improbable feature of the Black Guillemot is the striking difference between summer and winter plumages. The other auks become generally drabber, the blacks greyer and the whites duskier, but the Black Guillemot transposes almost to the photographic negative of itself in summer: the body white with contrasting mainly black wings.

Guillemot and Razorbill chicks leave the nesting cliffs before they are fully fledged, usually when they are about two-thirds grown. They have plenty of subcutaneous fat, and warm down covered by a layer of water-repellent body feathers, so that they can safely swim. Their 'wings' are mere stubs at this stage, which makes their early departure from the nest all the more amazing, as they jump off the ledges into the sea, which may be several hundred feet below! Despite their inability to fly properly, feathers and blubber combined seem to have a sufficient cushioning effect to allow them to bounce off the rock face on the way down without harm. The operation is made in one way more hazardous by taking place at night, but this at least allows the young birds a better chance of escaping the attentions of marauding gulls. Once off the cliff face, the chick swims with its parents, and often in the company of a group of other families, out to the open sea to complete its development away from the ever-present gull menace on the cliffs. Young Puffins are more mature when they leave the nesting burrows, but they too are vulnerable particularly to Great Black-backed Gulls; so they make their way to the sea under cover of darkness and independent of their parents.

The Manx Shearwater uses similar tactics to the Puffin, also to escape Great Black-backed Gull predation. Shearwaters, too, nest underground on remote and usually uninhabited islands. Most colonies are near the cliff top or close to the shore of low-lying islands, but a striking exception is the colony more than a mile from the sea and some 2,000 feet (600 m) up in the rocky screes in the centre of Rhum, one of the Inner Hebrides. By day, walking along the cliff top,

Manx Shearwater

there would be no reason to suspect that a Shearwater colony existed in the 'rabbit burrows' all round, but at night there can be no mistake. The eerie caterwauling, crowing calls of the adults underground and as they fly overhead in the darkness with a rush of air like the passage of a wartime shell are absolutely distinctive. The tremendous cacophony of the large Manx Shear-water colony on the Calf of Man is described in one of the Icelandic *Sagas*, and in Norway in the past their mysterious and terrifying chorus was attributed to angry trolls.

Actually the nest is often in a rabbit burrow — the luckless rabbits are quickly evicted — or otherwise dug by the birds themselves or set in a natural cavity in a scree. The parents feed the single youngster an oily, smelly but highly nutritious mixture of fish and plankton. On this it grows quickly, becoming very fat (and in itself nutritious — a related Australian shearwater, locally called the 'mutton bird', is still eaten by man). A couple of weeks before it is due to fledge it is far too heavy to fly. Its parents abandon it at this stage and return to the open ocean for the winter, while it converts its stored energy into muscle and completes its feather growth. After dark each night it emerges from its burrow for wing-flapping exercises, eventually slimming and maturing enough to leave on a moonless night and embark on its maiden flight, which will take it in due course to wintering grounds off Brazil.

Earlier in the breeding season, the adults will have changed over incubation duty, or come ashore to feed their chick (then clad in masses of fluffy grey down) only at night, to escape the savage butchery that Great Black-backs can exact as the clumsy Shearwaters struggle towards their burrows. The sitting bird may have been waiting a few days for relief when its mate returns from a fishing trip, and responds eagerly to the crowing, cooing calls as it passes overhead. Through long familiarity the pair will recognise each other's calls, so in this way even in the dark the right nest is quickly located. Their powers of navigation and homing are remarkable. Some years ago a female was taken off her egg in a burrow on Skokholm, and flown (in an aircraft) to Boston, USA, and there released. She had safely returned to her burrow before the letter detailing her liberation had reached the island.

As their name suggests, Shearwaters fly low, often touching the waves with a wing tip as they bank and turn. They are masters of energy-conserving flight, moving on long, narrow wings, held stiff, cutting at speed across the ocean air currents, gaining lift even off the waves, and flapping their wings only in still air. During the breeding season Welsh birds may regularly fish for food as far away as the Bay of Biscay. Returning birds will gather in huge 'rafts' offshore as dusk begins to fall.

Outside the breeding season, the two small petrels that breed in Britain and Ireland, Storm and Leach's, are just as much trans-oceanic wanderers as the Manx Shearwater, but their journeyings are the more remarkable because of their small size and apparently feeble, ineffectual butterfly-like flight. These, too, are nocturnal birds and fall prey also to the larger gulls. Occasionally other predators find a petrel colony and exploit it, though not usually making a devastating impact. Both Little and Short-eared Owls are known to do this, and the individual birds responsible can be quickly recognised because of their unkempt oil-smeared plumage and because they have acquired some of the musky odour characteristic of their prey.

The small petrels again are normally birds of uninhabited islands; the rats or cats so often associated with human habitations would make short work of them. Like so many hole-nesting birds, they lay rather rounder than the norm white eggs. Storm Petrels are widely distributed off our western and northern coasts, reaching as far south as the Isles of Scilly (and the Channel Islands), whereas Leach's Petrel is confined to a handful of remote islands in the extreme north. Both are tantalising species for the birdwatcher: being black (with only a small white rump marking) and coming ashore to reach a nest in a hole underground only during darkness is one problem, but their small size and erratic flight also makes them very difficult to spot amongst the waves when flying offshore in daylight. As with the Manx Shearwater, their nocturnal calls in the colony are a giveaway, and a delight. The Storm Petrel has a steady purring trill, whereas Leach's has a wild whooping whistle of a call, as bouncy as its flight. These calls are accompanied by emissions of a musky scent, and it has been argued that scent emission may act as an additional aid for the homecoming bird to find its mate. Although birds possess (so far as we can judge) the necessary structures and nerves for a sense of smell, they do not seem in general to exploit these powers. The petrel family is equipped with strange twin tubes over the nostrils and it is suggested that these help scent perception.

Although gull-like in its white and grey plumage, a close-up view shows that the Fulmar has a more complicated beak than a gull, formed of several segments with the joints between them clearly visible. On the ridge of the beak lie the two tubes which indicate that the Fulmar, too, belongs to the 'tube-nose' or petrel family. Fulmars do not have the musty odour of the small petrels, and in their case it has been suggested that the tubes have a pressure-sensitive mechanism that allows them to function as an air-speed indicator in much the same way as does a Pitot tube on an aircraft.

Fulmars are master gliders, and their flight is another feature distinguishing them from the gulls. Their stiff, narrow wings are held slightly downturned, like some modern jet fighters, and their dumpy but well-streamlined bodies allow them to plane along, skimming close to the waves, exploiting every chance of cheap energy in much the same way as Manx Shearwaters. Even their eyes are deep-set in the feathers of the head, and the feet are usually tucked out of sight within the body feathers for better streamlining. Only close to the nesting cliffs do they extend their feet and use the webbing between the toes for fine adjustments in manoeuvring.

93

The history of the Fulmar in Britain and Ireland is very much a success story. In the latter part of the nineteenth century they were restricted to remote St Kilda, off the Outer Hebrides, where the islanders depended heavily on them. They were 'farmed' sensibly for food (eggs, young and adults were all eaten), for oil (to light the lamps, fuel the cooking stoves and for general medicinal purposes) and for feathers (both for domestic use and for 'export', to help pay the rent when used to stuff army pillows). An expansion took place, first to equally remote Foula, and subsequently to other northern islands. During this century there has been a steady southwards spread, and the coasts of Britain and Ireland are now completely ringed by Fulmar colonies. Even where there are no cliffs, like the Dungeness shingle peninsula in Kent, they take the next-best manmade alternative: in the case of Dungeness, the nuclear power-station windowsills. Obviously, this is an adaptable bird!

What, however, caused the population explosion? Probably a combination of their opportunism, their biology, and the activities of man. They seem to have exploited first the rise of the whaling industry in the North Atlantic, and, when that failed, transferred their attentions to the expanding fishing fleet. Increasingly, fish were salted and more recently frozen, necessitating gutting at sea, and the Fulmars fed voraciously on the offal thrown overboard. Biologically, although it is thought that most Fulmars do not breed until they are seven or eight years old, many will survive as breeding birds for perhaps thirty years or more (even outliving the high-quality alloy rings that we put on their legs to see how long they live!). So, even if they only lay one egg each year (which is usually the case) it is hardly surprising that Fulmars are on the increase, as only two of those eggs need to reach maturity for the population to remain stable.

Perhaps their aggression also helps Fulmars to survive. They usually choose broad ledges for nesting, as they are clumsy on land and need adequate space for take-off and landing. Although nowhere near as noisy as Kittiwakes, they have a display chorus that sounds rather like a choir of crooning chickens. They defend themselves well, spitting quantities of foul-smelling oily stomach contents at intruders who approach the nest too closely. This they can do with accuracy — even nestlings just a few days old — at a range of several feet. Once polluted, the birdwatcher's clothing never loses the tell-tale aroma. On the wing, Fulmars will go for potential predators near the nest, even those as large as Ravens and Sea Eagles, and occasionally also startled and discomfited rock-climbers or innocently straying sheep. The technique is very effective: once hit, the offending bird lands and starts to preen furiously, trying to get its plumage back into shape.

Although by no means so aggressive, except to next-door neighbours of their own kind in the nesting colony, Gannets are also one of the seabird success stories of this century. In the old days, they too were 'harvested' by island communities, and even today a special provision in the law allows the islanders of our own Sula Sgeir to take an annual harvest of young Gannets, called 'gugas'. There are now 18 occupied gannetries in Britain and Ireland, no less than 11 of them founded this century. Most are on remote islands or stacs, but two (on Grassholm, off Pembrokeshire, and on Bass Rock, off Berwickshire) are fairly accessible and feature amongst outings offered by local boatmen. A third, Bempton Cliffs in Yorkshire, is exceptional in that it is on the mainland and fairly well south on the east coast. Bempton is an RSPB reserve, and although access is to a degree controlled for the protection of both the birds and the visitors, this is by far the easiest place to see Gannets on their nesting ledges.

The world population of the Gannet has trebled this century, and with some

Gannet

140,000 breeding pairs Britain and Ireland hold 70 per cent of the world population. Perhaps as much as one third of the world total now nests on Boreray and its associated stacs, which is part of the St Kilda group. This is the largest northern hemisphere gannetry, perhaps the largest in the world, and may now hold over 60,000 pairs. At a distance, the towering cliffs (at their lowest, several hundred feet clear of the sea) are so Gannet-encrusted that they look like a giant iced cake, snow-white with the birds and their guano.

This colony must rank as one of the seven modern visual wonders of the bird world, and the spectacle can be imagined when hundreds of Gannets are plunging headlong into the waves, often from 100 feet (30 m) or more, in pursuit of a school of fish. How there are not more collisions is difficult to understand, as birds are plummeting in from all directions at high speed, then bouncing back to the surface, heavily laden with fish, for a laborious take-off run pattering across the waves. An adult Gannet, or indeed its well-grown single youngster, may take up to a couple of pounds (1 kg) of fish in a meal. Some mental arithmetic on the daily catch of fish when the Boreray colony is in full swing indicates that a prodigious 200 tons or more of fish a day are needed to supply it!

Cormorants and Shags, though taking much the same sizes of fish as the Gannet, are nowhere near so spectacular. They, too, hunt underwater, but closer inshore, and submerge with scarcely a ripple from swimming on the surface, rather than entering the water in a spectacular splash. Feeding in shallow waters, they are able to include flatfish from the sea floor in their diet as well as mid-water species.

Both Cormorant and Shag are widespread around the coasts of Britain and Ireland, but seem to avoid competition for resources at least in part, on a basis of size, the larger Cormorant taking rather larger fish. Elsewhere in the world, such a distinction has been turned to commercial advantage in the past (and persists, as an anachronism, even today) by Japanese fishermen who employed a special 'guild' of bird catchers to take the largest species, the Japanese Cormorant, from its cliff nesting colonies because it was capable of catching bigger fish than the others. These 'domesticated' cormorants were held by long lines attached to collars, which both prevented their escape and stopped them actually swallowing the fish, and were set to dive for fish from their master's small boat. In keeping with current industrial trends, these working cormorants were allowed regular rest periods, during which they perched on the gunwale of the boat, wings outstretched. This wings-outstretched posture is to be seen regularly in their wild cousins as, strange as it may seem, the plumage of Cormorants and Shags is not well waterproofed with natural oils, and routine drying-off rest periods are necessary, otherwise the birds might become waterlogged, with disastrous results. With the fossil record of the cormorant family stretching back at least 30 million years, it could be argued that their evolution is progressing rather slowly!

Our Cormorant, the 'Great Cormorant' of almost world-wide distribution, is a bird of most coastal areas, whether the water is clear or murky, shallow or deep, whereas the Shag is more numerous in the clear, deep waters off rocky western and northern coasts. There are nesting differences, too. The Cormorant, though occasionally nesting on cliff ledges, usually chooses low, flat-topped islets, while the Shag prefers well-protected ledges or cavities deep beneath boulder tumbles, sometimes a long way above the sea. To the sensitive nose, most seabird colonies have a powerful and often unpleasant smell, but the Shag must come close to the top of any league table based on unpleasantness. There can be few birdwatching experiences so disquieting as to wriggle on your stomach into an occupied Shag nesting cavity, not knowing whether your intrusion is going to be greeted with a volley of half-digested regurgitated fish or half a bucketful of evil-smelling whitewash!

Such a 'whitewash' of droppings is also a conspicuous indicator of Kittiwake nesting colonies, and evil-smelling though it is nowhere is its tacky consistency put to better use. The nest is about 1 foot (30 cm) in diameter, and made of mud, seaweed fragments and a colourful variety of oddments of flotsam and jetsam, all cemented together with liberal quantities of tacky droppings. Kittiwakes are strongly colonial, often with hundreds of pairs gathering and their raucous cries of 'kitti-wa-a-a-ke' readily leading the birdwatcher towards their chosen site. This is usually on a sheer cliff face on rocky stretches of coast or on offshore islands. A good definition of a Kittiwake nest site would be that no other bird could nest there, as the slightest of projecting rocks, even under a tremendous overhang, serves as a foundation to which the nest can be stuck. Kittiwake youngsters, usually one or two in number, are much less mobile than the chicks of most of their gull relatives. This 'specially good behaviour' is totally logical, as until they fly they cannot walk more than a few inches from where they hatched, no matter how hungry they are, nor how anxiously they watch a food-carrying parent flying past, waiting to choose the right moment to land in the turbulent air currents against the cliff face. If they fall from the nest, it is to their doom.

Like Fulmars, Kittiwakes are currently successful birds. As a demonstration of their versatility, in areas lacking suitable cliffs Kittiwakes readily resort to man-made alternatives, and there are several colonies on pier ledges and waterfront warehouse windowsills. Kittiwake colonies are often easy to watch, from a sensible distance using binoculars to bring the action into close-up, and few hours of birdwatching will be more interestingly spent. Their nests are so close together that in the hurly-burly of comings and goings at the colony any real fighting could easily dislodge eggs or young and send them tumbling into the seas below. Instead of fighting, Kittiwakes seem to specialise in hurling abuse at their neighbours if they venture too close. Each time an adult returns to the nest, there is an effusive and vociferous greeting display to watch, with much head bowing and wing flapping.

Small and slender for a gull, the Kittiwake is elegant with black legs and vermilion-lined yellow beak. It is a marvel that these graceful birds will leave their colonies in July to spend the winter spread around the Atlantic Ocean, as far afield as the iceberg waters of the Newfoundland Banks. The sound of breaking waves must accompany Kittiwakes all their lives, as much a feature of the stormy ocean in winter as it is at the foot of their nesting cliffs. Although they may owe some of their success to man's fishing activities, they remain essentially 'sea gulls', free from some of the less pleasant features of the other gulls, many of which maintain an association with man throughout the year.

Of all the seabirds it is the gulls that are nature's generalists and most adept at coexistence with man. This is very much the century of the rise of the gulls, so it is strange to think that at the turn of the century they were rare birds inland — hence the term 'seagull'. Now they are as much a part of farmland as lapwings, as much a part of urban life, on playing field or rubbish tip, as blackbirds and starlings. It would be difficult to spend a day anywhere in Britain and Ireland without seeing numbers of several gull species, and the sight of straggling V formations heading for the coast or a nearby lake or reservoir is commonplace towards dark.

What is the reason for this change? It is probably that gulls exhibit great versatility in feeding, which has led to changes in distribution and numbers. The smaller gulls (Common and Black-headed) exploit the opportunities offered by farming: following behind the plough and eating earth-worms and other soil animals is a good example. All the gulls exploit refuse, the visible and to gulls edible evidence of man's increasing affluence during this century. In winter, no town rubbish tip is likely to be without a scrabbling mass of gulls searching the refuse for food.

The Black-headed is the only gull that really exploits the breeding possibilities of the low-lying coasts of south-east England, nesting sometimes in huge colonies on estuary islands largely protected from disturbance by extensive mudflats. Further north, it nests readily on coastal sand dunes or in marshy areas beside the lochs of hill regions. The Common Gull, though with outposts in the south, is a northern species, breeding on grassy moorland and low rocky islets in Scotland and Ireland. The Herring Gull (which remains with us all year) and the Lesser Black-backed Gull (which migrates south for the winter) are closely related, and breed on the cliffs or cliff tops in the west and north. If sheer increase in numbers is a sign of success, then Herring Gulls, currently expanding at the phenomenal rate of 10 per cent per annum, must be considered to be extremely successful. Most nest on rocky cliffs, sufficiently towering to be undisturbed by man, but in the far north and west they will often breed on low rocky islets or sand dunes. Sometimes pairs are widely scattered, but where the numbers to be accommodated are large and the available sites few, huge dense colonies will form. There are now a number of island colonies of both species in remote moorland areas, and many instances of Herring Gulls breeding on roof-tops in coastal towns. This habit started in Dover in the 1920s, and quickly

Herring Gull

spread. The raucous 'dawn chorus', starting soon after midnight in the height of summer, and the liberal aerial bombardment and occasional physical attacks on unsuspecting holidaymakers has led to a sharp fall in the seagull's popularity! Despite this, many Herring Gull nests allow admirable opportunities for study-ing the intricacies of bird behaviour. The speckled grey youngsters can be seen to solicit food by wheedling cries and an obvious begging posture. No matter how persistent they are, all this will be of no avail until the chick pecks at the red spot clearly visible on the tip of the adult's yellow beak. This stimulus triggers the feeding response, and the parent promptly disgorges a meal. This may seem to be a needlessly stereotyped behaviour pattern, but very clearly it is successful.

Largest of the gulls, the Greater Black-backed Gull is also a secluded cliff or undisturbed island nester, only rarely colonial, and then the colonies are small. Greater Black-backs can develop into birds of prey, seizing an unfortunate Puffin as it emerges (temporarily blinded by the light) from its burrow. A few savage blows from the beak and the Puffin is despatched, skinned and eaten in a single mouthful. On occasion, they will even fly down Petrels, Shearwaters or

Puffins, grabbing them in mid-air and even devouring them while still in flight. Herring Gulls are more subtle, loitering among the Puffin burrows and apparently devoting their attention to one particular adult circling offshore with a beakful of small fish for its nestling. Puffins are not the most skilful fliers among seabirds, and find manoeuvring difficult. On a windy day, the added harassment caused by a waiting gull leads, often enough, to misjudgement and a crash landing. In the resultant confusion the fish are dropped, to be picked up by the gull at leisure after the Puffin has beaten a retreat.

More sinister, the gull population explosion and the increasing size of gulleries is putting considerable pressure on other coastal birds, desiring to nest in the same habitat but lacking the gull's size, power and aggression. Many tern colonies in particular are threatened in this way as the terns are forced off their favourite beaches. Finding an effective and acceptable techique to stem the advance of the gulls is a problem in many coastal nature reserves. When the need is to eliminate a few rogue pairs of Great Black-backs the solution may be relatively simple, but when several thousand pairs of Herring Gulls are the root of the problem adequate control of them may be no easy matter.

Principal victims of the gulls' expansion are the terns. Aptly deserving their popular name 'sea swallows', the terns are perhaps the most graceful of our sea-birds. Most are considerably smaller, shorter legged and slimmer even than the Black-headed Gull, their silver-grey and white plumage offset by darker wing tips and a black cap. The dagger-like beak varies from black and black-and-yellow to blood red in the various species that breed in Britain and Ireland. All are migrants, travelling to fish in the oceans of the southern hemisphere during the winter, returning to our coasts to breed in summer. All the terns are colonial breeders, and the colonies may be thousands strong, so their displacement may have a profound effect on tern numbers, not just here but in the North Atlantic as a whole. Often tern colonies are located on remote beaches and sand dunes, or on small islands offering the greatest security from human disturbance and from predators such as foxes, rats and (astonishingly) hedgehogs, which have a taste for eggs. Eggs and young alike offer some of the most perfect examples of camouflage to be found in the bird world, and are nearly invisible against the background of sand flecked with fragments of seaweed or shell. In the case of the smallest and scarcest, the Little Tern often breeds in the south and east on beaches popular with holidaymakers, and besides suffering almost continuous disturbance in fine weather may lose eggs or young to the feet of unwary trippers.

Of the other terns, Common, Arctic and Sandwich in particular can be seen from spring to autumn feeding close inshore in many coastal areas, including those near to popular holiday resorts. The standard tern fishing technique is to flicker along lazily in the air a few feet above the waves before suddenly turning and plunging headlong into the sea with an audible 'plop' and a considerable splash. The tern penetrates only a few inches rather than submerging deeply. Their prey is usually small fish or shrimps, and these are either eaten on the spot or taken, one at a time, back to the colony to feed the young. Early in the season, the male will often bring a fish back to his mate, standing guard at the shallow saucer-shaped scrape in the sand that will serve for a nest. Although the colonies may seem close-packed, terns are vociferously abusive neighbours, squabbling frequently, and closer inspection will reveal that the nests are always at least two beak-thrusts apart.

The Arctic Tern, as its name suggests breeding largely in northern Britain and Ireland, probably sees more hours of daylight each year than any other creature. They breed well up into the Arctic Circle, where the summer is virtually nightless, and having raised their young on fish and the summer abundance of insect larvae, migrate southwards across the Equator. They spend our winter in the Antarctic Ocean, where once again they have the benefit of almost perpetual daylight and can enjoy an immensely rich food supply of small fish and plankton. With an annual migration of this magnitude, Arctic Terns must be amongst the avian long-distance record holders. The oldest Arctic Tern that we know of was a ringed bird that lived for 26 years. Travelling almost from pole to pole twice each year, its lifetime mileage is unthinkably high — certainly several million miles.

The terns are also the major target of another group of gull relatives, the skuas, that have predation or parasitism as their main way of life. Two of them are only seen occasionally around our coasts: the Long-Tailed Skua, little bigger than a Sandwich Tern but with very long central tail feathers, is a rarity; but the Herring Gull sized Pomarine Skua, with thick blunt-ended and twisted elongated central tail feathers, although scarce, is a regular passage migrant in several areas, particularly in late spring in the English Channel. The other two breed in Scotland, particularly in remote parts of the Hebrides, Orkney and Shetland, migrating south to equatorial waters for the winter. The Great Black-backed sized Great Skua, brown and bulky, with the central tail feathers only just projecting beyond the rest of the tail, is best recognised from juvenile gulls by the large white patch in the centre of each wing. The Arctic Skua, Common Gull sized, has central tail feathers projecting a few centimetres, and to make identification more difficult comes in a variety of plumage 'phases' ranging from a buffish body with dark cap and wings to chocolate-brown all over; all phases, however, have a bold white wing patch.

Arctic Skuas are slender-winged and extremely agile in flight. They will harass (sometimes singly, sometimes as a team) terns, Kittiwakes or the smaller gulls, relentlessly chasing their victim until it drops or disgorges the food it is carrying. So quick in flight are they that normally they will swoop to catch the dropped items before they reach the sea. A similar form of piracy is practised by the Great Skua, a slower and more ponderous flyer, which will chase most gulls and terns and even Gannets. Sometimes physical violence is used, and a favoured Great Skua tactic is to seize the Gannet's wingtip, in flight, and throw it off balance. Bigger though they are, Gannets are not nimble in flight and cannot tolerate such treatment. Great Skuas extend parasitism to predation on many occasions, and can be even more vicious than Great Black-backed Gulls in dealing with Petrels, Shearwaters and Puffins.

Two other groups of birds — the waders and the ducks — are regularly seen in coastal areas. Ducks and waders feature elsewhere in this book, but a few are largely restricted to sea coasts and thus merit consideration here. Long expanses of sandy beach right round Britain are characterised during the winter months particularly by the Sanderling, a neat silver-grey and white wader about the size of a Song Thrush. Sanderlings feed on small animals disturbed along the edges of the waves sweeping up onto the sand, scampering along so quickly that their black legs seem just a blur as they dash out after a receding wave only to rush back up the beach as the next wave follows. Rocky shores, and thus particularly the north and west coasts, and again primarily from autumn through to spring,

Turnstones and Purple Sandpipers

are characterised by two other waders, the Turnstone and the Purple Sandpiper. Turnstones, chequered black, white and chestnut, and very well camouflaged against rocks and seaweed, use their flattened beaks as shovels, sometimes, as their name suggests, to overturn stones to reach the small marine animals beneath but more often to seek maggots and the like in the old seaweed left on the tide line. Purple Sandpipers probe for food amongst the seaweed on the rocks, right in the splash zone of the breaking waves; they are a high-Arctic breeding species, commoner in winter in the north of Britain than in the south.

Of the group of ducks largely confined to the sea, the most characteristic and the most widespread is the Eider. Eiders breed on deserted stretches of coastline and on many off-shore islands in the north and west of Britain and Ireland, the females relying on their camouflage and absolute stillness to escape detection by predators. In his black and white plumage, the male is as obvious as his female is inconspicuous, but as is normal among the ducks he takes no part in incubating the eggs or rearing the brood of ducklings. The warm down with which the female lines and insulates her nest is exploited in Iceland and elsewhere to provide the filling for 'eiderdowns' and sleeping bags, and the French name for the bird, *duvet*, indicates a similar usage there. Eiders feed a great deal on shellfish such as mussels, and are currently on the increase. They dive for their food and may now be met with in winter in almost any coastal waters.

The same is true of the Common Scoter, though there are small breeding colonies in Scotland and Ireland. Considerable winter flocks may build up in suitably sheltered bays round our entire coastline, where adequate food supplies exist — again mostly shellfish. The male Scoter is black all over, the female sooty brown, and because of their habit of flying in line astern low over the seas these are among the easiest of ducks to identify even at long range. Occasionally amongst the long lines of dark birds will be seen one with flashing white wing patches — this is the much scarcer Velvet Scoter.

There remains the Long-tailed Duck, small and neat, and a feature particularly of Scotland's east coast. The creamy white and brown plumage of the Long-tailed Duck changes in pattern quite dramatically from summer to winter, and as they are present in northern waters in most if not all months any stage may be seen. Identification might pose some problems were it not for its size, habitat and, often enough visible, the male's extremely long tail.

Thus, overall, the conclusions that can be drawn indicate that coastal areas hold most birds, and are of most use to birds in the fullest ecological terms, during the summer months. For the birdwatcher, this means that the breeding season is the time to enjoy the spectacle that this habitat provides, and the time to derive most interest from more intensive observations or studies, rather than just 'looking'. It is worth remembering that, for many seabirds, attendance at the breeding colonies can begin early in the year, with birds regularly on the cliffs on warm days even before spring has started. Equally, for most species, the breeding season is all but over when we elect to take our national summer holidays; by August, many birds will have departed to the open seas for the winter.

Rocky coasts, because of the underlying geology of Britain and Ireland to be found predominantly in the west and north, hold by their nature much more birdlife than low-lying coasts in the south and east, but this may be more true in the breeding season than during the winter. The more sheltered location of, for example, the Channel coast in winter compared with the gale-swept western rocky shores, may allow more seabirds to remain inshore during the winter months.

7 Rarities

Although we now know a great deal about the routes that they take, the hazards that they face on the journey, and how they obtain the energy to fuel sometimes phenomenal feats of endurance, the major marvel of bird migration — how they navigate — remains a largely unsolved mystery. Research workers, using magnets to alter electrical fields, mirrors to change the angle of the sun or a planetarium to reorientate the night sky star pattern have amply demonstrated that birds can navigate with accuracy in many circumstances. Just how this system works, however, with its need for precise measurement of angles and an accurate timing system, integrated with goodness knows what else to form the most compact yet complete navigation complex known to man, remains as perhaps the greatest unsolved biological problem. Clearly, the navigation system must be contained in the bird's brain, and with many long-haul migrants (navigating with pinpoint accuracy to the same copse or reedbed both in Britain and in Africa in subsequent seasons) weighing in total half an ounce or even less, the degree of miniaturisation involved is almost unbelievable.

Bird migration has been an accepted natural phenomenon since man first put pen to paper, fascinating the ancients as much as it intrigues us today. Some of the earliest references are in the Old Testament of the Bible, for example in the *Song of Solomon:* 'For lo, the winter is past, the rain is over and gone. The flowers appear on the earth; the time of the singing of birds is come, and the voice of the turtle is heard in our land.' The 'turtle' referred to is of course *not* the voiceless marine reptile but the Turtle Dove. Over the centuries dispute has raged as man has become more 'scientifically' interested in his surroundings as to how the migrants navigated and where they went in winter. As recently as 300 years ago, swallows and martins were still thought by some to overwinter in the mud at the bottom of ponds.

There are a few places where migration is just so obvious that no one could fail to notice what is going on; an excellent example is the concentration of tens of thousands of birds of prey and storks crossing the narrow waters of the Bosphorus, *en route* between Europe and Asia and Africa. Another is the autumn gatherings of thousands of birds of prey at Falsterbo, in southern Sweden, prior to crossing the narrow straits separating Scandinavia from the

Arctic Terns on migration (see p. 101)

main European land mass. Inspired by the information that could be gathered in such circumstances, other early migration observation points were set up, manned by a few enthusiastic pioneers such as Eagle Clarke in the early years of this century. These were coordinated by no less than the British Association for the Advancement of Science, and tended to be situated on islands, headlands, isolated lighthouses and lightships that seemed to lie on natural north-south flyways. The modern bird observatories are located in very similar places.

The first bird observatory proper was founded by one such enthusiastic amateur, Heinrich Gatke, who spent half a century on the now German (but then British) island of Heligoland, off the German North Sea coast, in the latter part of the nineteenth century. His account of migration through the island (*Die Vogelwarte Helgoland*) makes compelling reading even today, and although some of the birds may be much rarer the pattern of events is much the same.

Islands in general have several advantages as bird observatories. Often they have a lighthouse, which may attract night migrants, especially if the weather turns bad overnight. Such an assisted landfall may be salvation for the many birds to be seen in nearby bushes at daybreak, but unfortunately at some lighthouses many dazzled birds are killed by flying into the lantern or tower. Islands, too, have the benefits of being of limited size, and often have relatively few patches of suitable vegetation to shelter migrants — hence the birds can be easily located and counted and a pattern associated with time of year and weather can gradually be built up.

The first British bird observatory was founded on the Welsh island of Skokholm, off Pembrokeshire, by Ronald Lockley, whose family were the only inhabitants and farmed the island. This was in 1933, and the island remains today unfarmed but still an observation point, although ringing is no longer carried out there. Since then, and with several comings and goings, the network round the British and Irish coasts has grown, until some 14 observatories are represented on the Bird Observatories Council, able to offer accommodation to visitors interested in participating in their work. These are augmented by several less-formally-organised ringing stations. Many of the island observatories are slightly difficult to reach because of their remoteness, which may make them especially attractive to those really wishing 'to get away from it all', but others, such as Portland Bill in Dorset, Dungeness in Kent and Gibraltar Point in Lincolnshire, are within easy reach of centres of population (see Appendix).

So what does an observatory do? In most cases, the observatory area is carefully scanned to note arrivals, and a daily log is kept of migrant numbers and direction of movement. This can be exciting work, sometimes because of the sheer number of birds arriving or passing over (as with an autumn 'fall' of thrushes on the East coast), sometimes because a rarity from afar has appeared, blown off course. Located as they are in the best spots for migration watching, observatories seem to work like magnets to less usual birds as well as to the mass of common migrants. Fair Isle, in the Shetlands, sees an astonishing percentage of rarities from as far afield as North America and the Far East, and offers an experience rarely to be obtained elsewhere.

For most birdwatchers, there can be little doubt that there is some *cachet* in seeing a really rare bird. Fascinating as the daily comings and goings are of the various birds that are a routine feature or component of the life of our countryside, it is specially intriguing to marvel at the arrival of an alien and to delight in, and improve recognition skills from, its plumage. Situated as they are at the extreme west of Europe, Britain and especially Ireland (and the Isles of Scilly) are best situated to intercept lost or weather driven birds from North

107

America. A glance at the autumn weather maps, with depressions looking just like giant dartboards in the North Atlantic, shows how this occurs. Round the tops of those depressions sweep westerly winds, often reaching or exceeding 100 mph (160 kph) at high altitude. Should a powerful-flying American migrant such as a duck or wader get caught up in one of these jet-stream tail winds, the crossing ('power assisted' by the wind) of the Atlantic is well within its flight endurance capabilities. Hence there are numerous records of such birds each year, plus an astonishing number of smaller birds, that also manage to survive the journey. Although for most of these species sightings are few and far between and not even at the rate of one a year, others, such as the Pectoral Sandpiper, seem to be in the throes of something more positive. Records are now annual, sometimes in numbers, and increasing occurrences are reported further east in Continental Europe. Perhaps we are seeing Pectoral Sandpipers in an expansionist phase, attempting to be the first American bird to establish regular wintering grounds on this side of the Atlantic.

Nevertheless the west is far from being the sole source of our rare vagrants; less than one-third of the rare birds (those necessitating identification ratification by the British Birds Rarities Committee) come from North America. Britain and

Pallas' Warbler

Ireland (though holding fewer regularly-occurring species than many mainland European countries) do receive visitations of birds with a more easterly distribution, for example when periods of easterly winds drift those birds off course on their south-north migration pathways. Sometimes freak climatic conditions, with a single massive weather system stretching across Europe and Asia, can bring oriental or Siberian wanderers to our shores — the Chiff-chaff sized but more boldly patterned Pallas' Warbler, for instance. Pallas' Warbler had occurred only three times in Britain before 1958: in 1896, 1951 and 1957. An influx of 6 in 1963 was considered astonishing at the time, but paled into insignificance against 18 in 1968 and 13 in 1974. So 37 of 44 records since 1958 had been produced by freak weather conditions in just three of the autumns.

In the last 35 years, 83 species of birds have been added, as newcomers, to the British and Irish list. Of these 46 originate (broadly speaking) from the west, the Americas, and 37 from the east, the great land mass of Europe and Asia. That they should have been found and identified (often by no means an easy task) is a tribute to the enthusiasm and skills of the growing numbers of birdwatchers involved. It is rather too easy to dismiss an interest in rarities as a meaningless pursuit, and sadly there have been several cases in recent years when in the enthusiasm to see a rare novelty crops have been damaged, or, perhaps worse, when the survival of a tired vagrant endeavouring to feed and recuperate has been jeopardised. That said, the broader aspects of a first sighting, or an early series of occurrences, should be kept in mind. The Pectoral Sandpiper is one case in point, of which the outcome is yet to be determined: has it opened up an east-Atlantic migration or not? In another case, that of the Collared Dove, there can be no such doubt.

Whatever may be thought of its habits, or the quality of its song, the rise of the Collared Dove is one of the most fascinating of bird success stories. Collared Doves are widespread, and often very numerous, in Asia and Africa. In the 1930s, for reasons not fully understood, but perhaps associated with a genetic mutation, an explosive expansion began. Collared Doves spread rapidly west-ward, establishing breeding populations as they went. By the mid-1950s they had reached Britain, and a pair bred in Norfolk in 1955, shrouded in intense secrecy. They bred again in 1956, joined by a few pairs elsewhere in south-eastern England. Strict secrecy was maintained, and local birdwatchers mounted guard on nest sites, straining eyes and ears for the signs that the nest (often deep in the gloom of an old cypress) had been successful. Looking back, with the bird as common as it now is, this episode takes on an almost comical aspect. In many parts of their range, Collared Doves are called Laughing Doves (perhaps they secretly enjoyed it all). Certainly, few concerned with the early records would have expected that in a decade the doves would have pest status in some southern counties because of their pillaging of grain and chicken food.

The Collared Dove seems always to be associated with mankind, especially in areas where grain is readily available. Most grain stores now have a resident population, as do most poultry farms. Interestingly, many of the early records in Britain were of birds closely associated with domestic chickens and the easy feeding available. Back in the mid-1950s, birdwatchers wondered just what

109

other species might be affected by the arrival of this unexpected newcomer to Britain. Would the Turtle Dove, similar in size, be displaced? However, when Collared Doves arrived, they found an 'ecological niche' not otherwise occupied: a situation ripe for exploitation. In the absence of competition, the next few years saw them demonstrate just how rapidly a bird population can expand. Certainly they seem able to breed in almost any month, even sitting shrouded in snow, and almost anywhere; there is even a record of a nest made of wire clippings built beside an electrical transformer. Apparently so far as can be judged, Turtle Dove populations have been quite uninfluenced by the new arrival. The only bird that might have suffered slightly is the Woodpigeon, in that its own expansion into our towns may have been halted by the Collared Dove's arrival.

Since the touchdown in Britain, Collared Doves have spread rapidly. They were breeding in western Ireland and in the Hebrides by the late 1960s. By 1970, or thereabouts, Iceland and the Faeroes had been reached and conquered, and a couple of years later they were recorded in Greenland! Where will it end? Such is the prodigious dynamism of the species that it may not be too rash to predict that, soon, Americans too might wake to the dry and unmelodious song of a new colonist.

Ross's Gull

It would be wrong to assume that all rare vagrants turn up at bird observatories; this is far from true, particularly of seabirds like the extremely rare Ross's Gull, a small gull breeding in the climatic harshness of north-eastern Siberia. Although there are still only a dozen or so records of Ross's Gulls, mostly from harbours in the north of Britain, the majority of these have been in the last decade and there may be a genuine increase in the occurrence of this delicate Arctic vagrant. However, the observatories remain by far the best place for the beginner to try his luck. Equally, it would be wrong to assume that the bulk of bird ringing, carried out (amongst other things) to help answer the questions surrounding the routes migrating birds take and their ultimate destinations, takes place at observatories. Bird ringers are widely distributed across Britain and Ireland, but it is again at the bird observatories that ringing is best demonstrated to newcomers. Most observatories operate ringing

Heligoland trap

programmes, using nets or large, permanent walk-in funnel-shaped traps built of wire netting over a line of bushes to catch the birds for marking, weighing and measuring. These traps are called 'Heligolands' after the first and very effective design built by Gatke on that island. The migration season runs from March to November, with only a brief midsummer lull, so there is much to be seen. In addition, some observatories have breeding seabird colonies, and others (such as Dungeness) are so situated that migratory movements of seabirds like skuas, terns and divers pass by close inshore, offering good views of birds notoriously difficult to see well.

Although the birds seen and ringed are only a small proportion of the vast migratory movements (some migrants fly only at night for example, and others usually far too high to be seen), the facts and figures produced by the concerted efforts of the bird observatories have helped enormously in understanding the paths migrants follow and their ultimate destinations. Their observations can be blended with those of research biologists using in some ways vastly more sophisticated study techniques like observing flight paths on radar sets. Radar observations have the benefit that night or day makes no difference to the 'seeing' power of the watcher, and of course they cover a far greater distance than can the human eye, so migrants coming into southern England in spring can be detected and traced from the French coast or before. They do suffer from two disadvantages, however: it is difficult to be sure how many birds are involved in creating each radar 'blip' that is followed, and although broad categories (large, middling, or small birds) can be used, precise identification of species is rarely possible.

When it comes to rare breeding birds, the situation is very different. For a start, most are still tragically vulnerable to the desires of egg-collectors, and all are specially protected by law not just against these egg-collectors but against disturbance by anybody, even an interested and dedicated naturalist. It is the role of conservation bodies (the Royal Society for the Protection of Birds and the Nature Conservancy Council in particular) to make the arrangements necessary to protect such birds. Sometimes the best protection is just complete secrecy concerning the event — not too difficult if the bird is small, relatively quiet and skulking and lives either in remote country or dense cover; the Temminck's Stints that occasionally breed on the wilder moors of Scotland are a good example. In other cases (for example the small group of Bee-eaters that bred in a Sussex sandpit in 1955) the birds themselves may be so tunefully noisy and brilliantly coloured that secrecy is out of the question and a round-the-clock guard of wardens has to be arranged. Because of the threats from egg-collectors and falconers, many Peregrine nests are wardened until the young fledge, and the English Golden Eagles are also wardened, though more to protect them from accidental and quite innocent disturbance by hill walkers.

One species to have made an exciting come-back from extinction in Britain and to liven up the sometimes rather dull Highland lochs is the Osprey.

Persecuted into extinction in the nineteenth century by gamekeepers, egg-collectors and skin-collectors, Osprey fortunes in Scotland took a turn for the better in 1954, when breeding was re-established, probably by an overspill from the flourishing and expanding Scandinavian population. Rigorous protection was, and sadly still is, needed to save the birds from egg-collectors, but the RSPB immediately stepped in to provide this. It is both a tribute to and a sad reflection on our times that sophisticated electronic devices should be used to protect nests of such rare species, but that also, on occasion, egg-collectors may succeed in avoiding the counter-measures and escape with the eggs. Despite the occasional

Osprey

mishap, the small population has grown, and there are now numerous successful bulky twig and branch nests in Scots pines in the Highlands. On many large rivers and lochs, the Ospreys themselves are to be seen through the summer months indulging in their spectacular dives for fish, often submerging in a shower of spray, before surfacing and flying off with a sizeable fish held (pointing fore-and-aft like an airborne torpedo) in the grip of savagely sharp talons and sandpaper-like toes. This is an excellent example of the benefits that can come from *not* concealing the presence of a rare breeding bird, but instead carefully controlling access and allowing viewing at a safe distance, from a hide with specially powerful binoculars. Apart from the success of the Ospreys themselves, the publicity value is inestimable to the conservation movement in general.

Given wide public support and, above all, financial backing, the conservation bodies are able to take the rather broader approach and protect not just the single pair at their breeding site but sufficient appropriate habitat to encourage permanent establishment. Normally this would imply the creation of a nature reserve on land either purchased or leased for the purpose, and striking examples are to be seen in the RSPB wetland reserves at Minsmere and Leighton Moss, where some of the rarest marsh birds have established safe strongholds, or the Havergate Island reserve. This was created, physically, following the disastrous 1953 east coast floods, to establish a breeding site suitable for Avocets — the RSPB emblem. The task was successfully accomplished, obviously to the benefit of the newly-formed and now flourishing Avocet population, but also generating much goodwill and good publicity for practical conservation.

A wide range of reserves now exists across Britain and Ireland, run by a large variety of conservation bodies, covering most habitats. Some are of local interest, others of national or international importance. In almost all cases some habitat management must take place to maintain the *status quo* (to prevent a reedbed turning into an alder carr, for example) and the general aim is to so operate the reserve that its inhabitants may be observed. This may not always be possible, of course, if, for example, sensitive birds choose to nest close to a path; in such cases it has to be remembered that the reserves are established primarily to protect birds and their habitat — not to provide easy viewing, although this, very often, is the bonus obtained. Visits to such reserves provide an excellent starting point for a closer look at birds of a particular habitat, and many of them are in naturally bird-attracting locations, or have been amended by ecologically-based landscaping to make them more attractive. Thus some, at migration times, may be as good a place to find rarities as any; the list of birds seen during the year at Minsmere and Stodmarsh (reedbed reserves in Suffolk and Kent respectively) pay eloquent testimony to this.

8 Into Europe

So far as birds are concerned, Britain, and Ireland even more so, are off-shore islands on the west of the Continental land mass. Islands the world over seem as a general biological rule to have fewer birds than the associated mainland; the reasons for this, like the shortage of habitats or sheer pressure of space, are easy to comprehend when the island is a small one. The rule still applies, though, to much larger islands, but possibly for different reasons such as the distance from the centre of the population, or differences (way back in history) in the timing of the separation of the island from that land mass. So Britain has fewer birds (species, that is) than the part of mainland Europe lying between the same degrees of latitude, and Ireland, further to the west still, has even fewer, with some striking absentees such as the Tawny Owl and Little Owl, the woodpecker family, and the Marsh and Willow Tits. Of course there are some compensating features: with a far greater coastline and access to far more fishing, our seabird populations are much superior to those on the Continent; and in winter, because the climate of Britain and Ireland is made considerably milder by the proximity of warm oceanic water currents, we see wintering masses of birds fleeing the savagely cold northern and central Europe.

Thus birdwatchers in Britain and Ireland see only a part of the full spectrum of bird life of the 'western Palaearctic', the zoogeographic region to which these islands belong. Our links, in zoogeographic terms, are clear and are governed mostly by temperature so far as breeding birds are concerned: we have many of the birds of the central latitudinal band of Palaearctic species, missing out, for example, on species as diverse as Great Snipe and Ruff (in most years), Eagle Owl and Black Kite, Black Woodpecker, Middle Spotted Woodpecker and

115

Wryneck (almost always), Crested Lark (common, it seems, right up to the Calais hovercraft terminal) and Bonelli's and Icterine Warblers. Even within England, this 'outpost of Europe' status is clearly evidenced by the species with a markedly south-east (and thus nearest to the Continent) bias. There are quite a number of these, but Woodlark, Black Redstart, Nightingale, Reed Warbler and Cirl Bunting give a broadly-based range of examples.

Some European species, such as Cetti's and Savi's Warblers, the Dartford Warbler and the Golden Oriole, have a tenuous toe-hold as breeding birds in Britain and thus *can* be seen here. Numbers are so small and protective measures often so strict on reserves, however, that they are difficult to see, and indeed if too many birdwatchers set out to see them sheer disturbance caused by people pressure could easily become a threat to their survival. There are strong arguments, too, in favour of viewing such birds in the numbers that they reach (which makes it so much easier to see them well in relaxed circumstances) in their natural habitat and range, rather than in what may be 'make-do' habitat at the extreme edge of their range.

Thus to get the full picture of European birds, and how the birds of Britain and Ireland are related to them, the birdwatcher should best plan to travel. So far, most mention has been made of the 'central latitudes' of Europe paralleling those spanned between the south coast of England and the Shetlands, roughly 50-60°N, but Europe extends north to 75° and south to 35°, corresponding roughly to mean January temperatures of about −20°C and 17°C respectively, and mean July temperatures of about 5°C and 27°C. This temperature range, from Arctic to Mediterranean, is vast, and could be expected to (and does) produce a fascinating range of species.

What, then, of the north? As the traveller ranges northwards, there are several visual, and often spectacular, indications of changing habitat, leave aside a falling temperature. The spaces become more wide-open as the presence of man diminishes; there are more 'high tops' of mountain and moorland in the landscape, and the woods coalesce to form forests, often gigantic ones. The trees change, too, to a preponderance of birch and conifer. In the extreme north, they become stunted, no more really than bushes, with willow and birch predominating. Thereafter lies the tundra, treeless expanses of various grasses, sedges and mosses, with a few specialised hardy flowering plants amongst them.

Perhaps the dominant feature of the tundra, and to visiting naturalists the major problem and literal source of irritation, is the number of insects, many of them blood-sucking. The brief Arctic summer produces a sudden abundance of insects and their larvae, and it is on these that the majority of tundra-breeding birds depend in one way or another. Most

116

European waders breed in this zone, though margins are never precise in ornithology and some, such as Golden Plover and Dunlin, have recognisable races or sub-species that breed as far south as England, and others, such as the Dotterel, have tiny relic populations breeding at the very top of the highest Scottish mountains. In the north, the waders are in their best, most colourful, plumage and are genuinely gorgeous; there are so many examples that selecting a sample is invidious, but perhaps the most dramatic changes from greyness to glamour are seen in the Bar-tailed Godwit, the Knot, Turnstone and Sanderling. Despite the apparent brightness of colour, this rufous summer plumage remains for most species more than adequate for camouflage against the generally reddish hue of grass, moss and lichen, and for those (such as the Grey Plover, silver-speckled but with a striking black-and-white breast and belly) which remain conspicuous, this self-advertisement has clearly stood the test of evolutionary time.

When we see waders most, either during the winter or migrating south in autumn, they are clad in drab buffs, browns and greys, at best with a speckling of the russets, reds, blacks and oranges of summer feathers remaining. True, in spring, some of the northward-moving waders on the estuary may be coming into summer plumage, but their stay is so brief that only rarely can a bird in full summer plumage be enjoyed. Beneath this brevity of stay lie the secrets of success in these northerly breeding migrants. The Arctic summer, from the melting of the snows which comes late because of the severity of winter frosts and the depth to which the soil is frozen, through the period of insect abundance to the onset of snowfalls and gales, is astonishingly brief, spanning two to three months, sometimes less. With continuous summer daylight, plant growth is accelerated, and, as a by-product, birdwatching hours are greatly extended each day. Thus for the breeding birds to be successful, timing is of the essence. The apparent urgency of spring migration is quite real; they *must* arrive on their breeding grounds in good condition and in good time to set up territory and lay as soon as weather and food supplies permit.

Some species (the Sanderling is an example) may try to maximise their success by making two nests in quick succession, the male incubating the first clutch as soon as it is laid, the female then laying a second in another nest and herself incubating it. In others — notably the Dotterel and the Red-necked Phalarope — an even more sophisticated approach has evolved. The female in these two is rather larger and brighter than the male, which betokens a rare reversal (for birds) of the roles of the sexes. The male incubates the first clutch, which he has fathered, and cares for the chicks, driving off the female if she enters the feeding territory. Meanwhile she produces a second clutch, fathered by another male, who then assumes responsibility for incubating these eggs,

117

from start to finish, and rearing the brood. It is assumed that such a reversal frees the female from the efforts of incubation, nest protection and raising the family, allowing her to maximise her role as an egg producer during this short and often harsh summer.

Red-necked Phalaropes

Besides allowing excellent views of many of our waders, ducks and geese in their normal breeding habitat — giving additional interest in seeing birds in all the habitats of their year, and studying how they exploit them — pushing northwards into the tundra allows views of several birds that would only be met with once or twice in a lifetime of normal birdwatching in Britain and Ireland. Birds like the Snowy Owl and Gyr Falcon give away, by their white or near-white plumage, their northern origins, but others to be seen in the far north include the White-billed Diver, Lesser White-fronted Goose, King Eider and Sabine's Gull, whereas amongst the smaller birds there is the Arctic Warbler, the Red-throated Pipit, and the Little and Rustic Buntings, which share the northern latitudes with Lapland and Snow Buntings, two species regularly occurring in Britain and Ireland in winter.

The major predators of these windswept Arctic wastes, beside the Snowy Owl and Gyr Falcon, are Rough-legged Buzzards and Arctic, Pomarine and Long-tailed Skuas. For each of these, often widespread through the tundra zone, the life-style demonstrates the close relationship that exists between predator and prey. The Rough-legged Buzzard, unlike its West Country cousin, is adapted to ground nesting, and it and the Pomarine Skua (to be seen off our coasts as it migrates to and from its breeding grounds) are dependent largely on local supplies of lemmings and voles. The rodent population may vary greatly

118

from one year to the next, and the birds' breeding success follows these variations closely. In years of low rodent populations, breeding densities are low, and many pairs may not breed or have little success in their attempts to raise a family. In such lean years, Rough-legged Buzzards leave their breeding range much earlier than usual, and travel further south in greater numbers than normal. Nevertheless, the tundra is a big place, and in an environment so harsh and unpredictable birds may be widely scattered or few and far between, so careful planning of bird watching trips is essential, as is allowing adequate time to cover the ground when means of transport may be just as unpredictable as the climate or as few and far between as the birds!

Coming further south, to the birch and willow scrub and then the boreal forest regions, the same caveats apply about access and finding birds once you have reached the scrub or forest. What can be said is how worthwhile it may be. In the scrub areas are to be found secretive but spectacularly handsome birds like the Bluethroat, blessed too with a magnificent song, and the Thrush Nightingale, closely similar to, but not such a perfectionist songster as our own bird. The windswept more-grassy areas (almost wet steppe) have breeding Cranes, with their wild trumpeting cries and high-kicking display dances, whereas forest clearings with pools may hold the tree-nesting Goldeneye that winters off British coasts or on reservoirs, or Great Snipe, Terek and Marsh Sandpipers, very scarce vagrants to Britain and Ireland.

Just as important, like an endless sea of firs, larches and pines, the boreal forest zone marches across northern Europe into Asia. On its northern margins, the forest fizzles out into birch scrub, whereas to the south deciduous trees gradually become more numerous as temperate forest takes over. Even further north, however, the relentless acres of conifer are occasionally relieved by scattered stands of birch, aspen and alder, with an understorey of juniper and other fruiting bushes. In much the same way as an agricultural monoculture, the boreal forest can lack variety and in consequence support fewer species than the more diverse temperate woodlands further south. Some birds have adapted, but in general the pine forest is an austere habitat. Insect-eaters are uncommon, and the few that do occur move south quickly at the onset of autumn, when food becomes scarce.

Best adapted are those birds that feed on conifer seeds: the Pine Grosbeak, the Common, Two-barred and Pine Crossbills, and the Nutcrackers. In all but the leanest years, these are the permanent residents, varying in numbers in parallel to variations in the fruitfulness of the forest. Productivity of the conifers peaks to abundance every two or three years, with associated rises in bird numbers. If a poor year follows, then a large-scale exodus of birds seeking new habitat may occur, giving the periodic invasions (or 'irruptions') of western Europe by Crossbills, Nutcrackers and Waxwings. The Siberian Jay is a more permanent resident of spruce and fir forests. Siberian Jays, like the other crows, are omnivores, mixing various insects, small mammals, birds' eggs and young with fruit and seeds according to season, and they share with our Jay the tendency to cache food supplies (nuts, seeds and berries) in hollow trees for use later in the winter. Only if the weather is exceptionally severe will they leave the forest. Siberian Jays have an additional 'plus feature' for birdwatchers: they are amongst the most confiding of all birds (unlike the other crows) and although rarely seeing man show no fear of him.

These forests also support a tantalising range of owls, though these are by no means so confiding, and some, such as the minute Pygmy Owl, are often difficult to see in the dense treetops. Though not much bigger than a sparrow, the Pygmy Owl, weight for weight, is amongst the most ferocious, attacking thrushes and rats bigger than itself. There are two medium-sized owls that would be strange to British eyes, Tengmalm's (rather bigger than the Little Owl and with a strikingly spectacled face) and the Hawk Owl, the most northerly-ranging of the forest owls, with an unusually long tail and hawk-like appearance for an owl, and diurnal in habits, which suits it to the almost perpetual daylight of the Arctic summer. At the top end of the size scale are the giant Ural Owl, like a monster version of the Tawny Owl and behaving in much the same manner, and the even larger Great Grey Owl. Almost the size of an Eagle Owl, the Great Grey, conspicuously round-headed and with glaring yellow irises, depends on the forest population of rodents of all sizes for food, and as with so many of the Arctic or near-Arctic birds its breeding success varies widely from year to year in parallel with fluctuations in rodent populations.

Now let us focus our attention on southern Europe: the Mediterranean countries. Although there are relatively few birds confined solely to the Mediterranean, like Eleanora's Falcon, the Spotless Starling and a small but attractive group of *Sylvia* warblers, this is a rich and colourful habitat for birds, popular with birdwatchers because it offers so much to see that is of extreme rarity or accidental occurrence, as an overshooting or wind-drifted migrant, in Britain and Ireland. Not all of the Mediterranean countries are similarly rich in birds; in some (Italy, Cyprus and Malta come readily to mind) the pressures from huntsmen, shooting often enough for sport rather than for the pot, and bird-catchers are so severe that there is little left to be seen in some areas.

One feature of the Mediterranean basin is that most of the best-known areas are remarkably large tracts of land, not, as is common in Britain and Ireland, relatively small areas protected as reserves. Many of these areas would merit mention in any global list of best birdwatching: the Coto Donana, Andalucia and the Pyrenees in Spain; the Camargue and Alpilles in southern France; parts of Majorca; Lake Neusiedler in Austria; northern Greece, Crete; the Danube delta in Romania, and some parts of Turkey, such as the Bosphorus narrows and Lake Apolyont. Turkey sits astride the junction between Europe on one side and Asia on the other, and has some Asian birds to show for this such as the Smyrna Kingfisher, a large, handsome bird, dark chestnut on the front and electric-blue on the back, better described by the name it has in India, the White-throated Kingfisher, because of a broad white blaze down its breast.

In some ways, the Mediterranean serves as much as a recuperative area for birds as it does for people, playing host each spring and autumn to many, many millions of long-haul migrants. In spring, these are birds often exhausted after their long flight across the Sahara and the Mediterranean Sea, which must break their swift northward passage to recover. In autumn, with young birds joining the adults, there are many more mouths to be fed as the birds pause in the Mediterranean region to build up their fat reserves before heading south to their winter quarters. Set half-way between the searing heat of the tropics and the chill of northern Europe, the climate here is benign, with mild humid winters and warm dry summers. Though lapsing during the hottest and driest parts of summer (which it is adapted to survive) the vegetation grows, flowers and fruits for much of the year, and this, and the insect life also present year-round, helps to account for the Mediterranean's value to birds. Bird life is sparsest in mid-summer, the arid period, when most of the birds about will be of tropical origin and adapted to survival in the dry thorny scrub of *maquis*. Most of these will have bred during the luxuriant spring, and will depart early to the south, to be replaced by both short-stay migrants and a range of resident winter visitors, predominant amongst which are various thrushes, warblers and ducks, which join the year-round resident birds in finding a reasonable, and reliable, supply of insects, fruits and grasses sufficient to remove the need to journey further south for survival.

For many, it is the sheer spectacle of colour that is attractive in Mediterranean birds. The Hoopoe is perhaps the most ubiquitous of these; ginger-buff, with bold black-and-white wings and a spectacular fan-shaped crest, it feeds on ground insects and often allows a close approach before flopping away in hesitant flight. The nest, usually in a hollow tree, is unusually easy to find because it must be about the most obnoxiously smelly of any bird, worse even than the Kingfisher. Also hole-nesters are the Bee-eaters, specialist as their name implies in catching and killing (by beating against a branch or stone) bees, wasps and many other insects. So brightly and variously coloured are they that the Australians call their species of Bee-eater the Rainbow Bird, and the same is true of its European counterpart, which has as an added attraction a delightful call like a ripple of handbells. Bee-eaters nest in exposed banks of sandy soils,

121

Hoopoe

and there is a particularly attractive colony close to the old bridge near Arles, in the Camargue, the bridge made famous in oils by Van Gogh.

The Roller, a migrant to southern Europe (breeding much further north in the east of its range) from tropical Africa, is also an open-ground insect-eater. Rollers choose suitable bushes and wait for an insect to pass by on the ground beneath. Almost jay-sized, they are carnivores, eating not only beetles, grasshoppers and large preying mantids but also lizards, small rodents and occasionally birds. Azure-breasted and chestnut-backed when perched, the Roller reveals electric-blue wings as it swoops down onto prey, but these wings are best seen during the tumbling display flight that gives the bird its name. In marked contrast, both in habitat and colour, is the Golden Oriole, which occasionally penetrates as far as south-east England to breed in suitable summers. Thrush-sized, the male is strikingly gold and black, but is amazingly well camouflaged amongst the bright sun and shade-dappled leaves of its tree-top habitat, drawing attention to itself more often by its beautiful fluting call. The olive-green female is much less conspicuous as she sits on her nest, slung hammock-like between the twigs and one of the masterpieces of avian building.

Many of the places listed as especially noteworthy for birds in the Mediterranean region are wetlands, and it is here that the richness of species within the same family that characterises the south, but that we in Britain and Ireland lack, is perhaps most obvious. Take the heron family, for example: we have two regular species, the Grey Heron (or just 'Heron') and the much rarer Bittern, and most birdwatchers would be lucky to see just one of the egrets in a lifetime of birdwatching in Britain and Ireland. On the Mediterranean wetlands there are Grey and Purple Herons, Little Bittern and Bittern, Great White, Little and Cattle Egrets, Squacco and Night 'Herons' (though the last two more closely resemble the small egrets) — nine species against our two! With such a range, it becomes much easier to discern how species sharing a habitat manage to partition the resources within it to avoid undue competition. In the case of the heron family, it is food supplies that are partitioned; in the breeding season, not only do many of them nest in colonies but in company with other members of the family. As a simple example of how competition is avoided (over and above such evolutionary adaptations as longer legs allowing fishing in deeper water) the Night Heron has adapted to roosting during the day, and, with its large owl-like eyes allowing it to see well, feeds in the failing light of evening. Thus it does not compete with the Squacco Heron, which eats similar frogs and small fish, nor with the Cattle Egret, which has taken to feeding on lizards and grass-hoppers and the like on drier ground, often associating with wild game (or in Europe, cattle) as they disturb such prey as they walk through the grass. Such is the adaptability of the Cattle Egret that it is now a regular follower of the plough, just as are the gulls in Britain!

Perhaps the most spectacular of the wetland birds is the Greater Flamingo, best seen at its large breeding colony in the Camargue. Flamingoes are colour-ful, if slightly grotesque in a stately way, but have a sophisticated banana-shaped beak and 'upside-down' feeding technique: the beak is immersed in

Flamingoes

water, and the tongue, which fits tightly into a groove, works like a pump plunger to suck water in over the comb-like edges of the beak. Here small animals are filtered out of the water, transferred to the gullet and swallowed. Just as colourful, but often inconspicuous for all its size, is the Purple Gallinule, like a giant Moorhen. As would be expected for a reedbed habitat, there are

123

inconspicuous specialist species to be found — if with difficulty. Two are confined to the Mediterranean/Caspian Sea basin and nearby: the tiny Marbled Teal and the Moustached Warbler. Amongst other ducks in this zone (which is fabulously rich in waterfowl in winter as well as summer) is the colourful Red-crested Pochard, as striking as the Marbled Teal is discreet.

The Mediterranean basin has a brand of thorny scrub all its own, perhaps better known under its French name *maquis* — whence came the name of the wartime French resistance movement, whose members sought shelter in its impenetrable tangles. An interesting group of one of the warbler families also specialises in living in this habitat, and some are amongst the most ubiquitous and characteristic of Mediterranean birds. All lurk deep in the cover, but are inquisitive, emerging briefly into sight to inspect any intruders in their domain. In spring, they tend to be more visible as they emerge to sing, perched or in a jerky parachuting song-flight. All belong to the genus *Sylvia*, which also contains our familiar Whitethroat and Blackcap, and these too are Mediterranean residents. Most widespread of the exclusively Mediterranean species are the large Orphean Warbler, greyish, with a staring white eye and melodious, thrush-like song, the boldly black-capped Sardinian Warbler and the subdued but attractive, mouse-like Subalpine Warbler. The Dartford Warbler (of which we have a tiny outlying resident population on some of our remaining southern heaths) and the Spectacled Warbler occur in the west of the region, whereas two others are even more restricted in their distribution. Maramora's Warbler, clad all in grey, is the most sombre-plumaged of all, and occurs on the Balearic Islands, Sardinia, Corsica and Sicily. Ruppell's Warbler, attractively black and grey with a striking white moustache, breeds in the Aegean Sea region but is perhaps most easily seen on Crete.

The scrubland clothes rocky outcrops that climb into arid hill regions. Here those familiar with the Common Wheatear only will be impressed by the addition of the Black-eared Wheatear, but most strikingly enthused by the Black Wheatear, all black save for a typical wheatear inverted U white rump. Here Black Redstarts can be seen in typical scree habitat, even though they are so much a feature of Mediterranean town rooftops, and the inconspicuous Rock Sparrow, better identified by its white tail spots than its yellow throat patch, and elegant Rock Bunting move tantalisingly in and out of sight amongst the rocks. High up, too, may be Crag Martins, Alpine and Pallid Swifts, but all of these may also be found (like the Black Redstart) using towns as an acceptable substitute habitat! Bursts of tuneful, clear fluting song can usually be traced to one of the Rock Thrushes, perched high on a crag or rock buttress. The Blue Rock Thrush, slate blue all over, resides year-round in the Mediterranean basin, and tends to occur at lower altitudes, in arid regions and near the coast. The migrant Rock Thrush, easily distinguished by its orange-chestnut tail and breast, is slightly smaller and more of a mountain bird, breeding usually above 3,000 feet (900 m) in altitude and ranging considerably further to the north than its cousin.

It would be impossible to close a discussion of Mediterranean birds without reference to the host of birds of prey to be seen in the region. If the bird fauna of Britain and Ireland is impoverished in one particular field, it is the raptors. We have few, and only the Kestrel, Sparrowhawk and Buzzard are at all numerous, and then not universally so. Visits to the Mediterranean add hugely to our understanding; we have no vultures, but there are four species in the Mediterranean. The huge Griffon and smaller, pointed-tailed and almost always scruffy white Egyptian Vulture can be found with little difficulty, although the Lammergeyer will be much more difficult (Crete is a good island for them) and the largest, the Black Vulture, may now be extinct over much of the region. Amongst the eagles, the Golden is to be seen, joined in various places through the region by Bonelli's Eagle and Booted Eagle — very variable in plumage and an even greater challenge to correct identification than most in this notoriously difficult group — and by the Short-toed or Snake Eagle, very pale below and prone to hover, flapping clumsily. In summer, with luck, one may be seen taking a snake, hanging limply from its talons, back to its family in a tree nest. Not in the mountains, but usually on open plains or over marshland, the rare Imperial Eagle, as large or larger than the Golden Eagle, may be seen, particularly in southern Spain where there is a separate race of this species.

The Harriers are all present and often numerous on passage, but only Marsh (in large numbers) and Montagu's remain to breed. The inevitably richer insect life favoured by the warm climate encourages the smaller falcons, the Hobby widespread, the Lesser Kestrel less so but often conveniently found in small colonies on crags near to towns or even in church towers and the like. Eleanora's Falcon is confined to the Mediterranean mostly on remote islands. Larger than a Hobby but similarly long-winged, this dark grey (or pale grey in the 'pale phase' form) has developed a late breeding season, which allows it to capitalise on the supply of southbound migrants in autumn as the major food source for its chicks.

Although raptor migration across the Straits of Gibraltar is impressive, particularly in autumn, it is at the other end of the Mediterranean that the greatest raptor (and stork) migration spectacular occurs, at the Bosphorus. Birds of prey (and both Black and White Storks) depend greatly on rising currents of warm air to soar, saving energy on long migrations. Such upcurrents are negligible over water, so these birds seek always the shortest sea crossings available. At Gibraltar, the birds involved are almost entirely the

125

European breeding stock moving south from as far afield as Russia and Scandinavia to winter in Africa. At the Bosphorus, similar species breeding further to the east are joined by many birds (such as Spotted and Lesser Spotted Eagles, Red-footed Falcons, Tawny or Steppe Eagles and Levant Sparrowhawks)

Spirals of migrating raptors

from Asian breeding grounds, and by mid-morning in August and September, given favourable weather, thousands, sometimes tens of thousands, and occasionally hundreds of thousands, can be seen in spirals over the mosques of Istanbul, gaining height before gliding down across the narrows, there, on the Asian side, to spiral again in the upcurrents rising off the hot dry hillsides, before setting off south towards Africa.

9 Globe Trotting

If travelling within Europe offers to the birdwatcher an increase in the scope and interest of the birds he watches and the habitats he explores, how much greater must be the fascination of birds viewed on a world scale. Only a couple of decades ago, to suggest the possibility of world travel in search of birds would have seemed far-fetched, if not laughable, but now (thanks largely to the modern travel network of which we may sometimes be over-critical) it comes as no surprise, and indeed many birdwatchers are doing just this. The arguments in favour of travel remain much the same: the knowledge and understanding of the kingfisher family (say) derived from comparing and contrasting the life-styles of about 90 species must surely be far more fascinating than, and complementary to, even a most detailed study of just one. The kingfishers are divided into two subfamilies, one containing the waterside birds that are familiar all over the world. The other contains the forest kingfishers, and it may come as a surprise to discover that this latter group is much larger and far more diverse in its adaptations. Fishing kingfishers have strong, narrow, sharp-pointed beaks, whereas the more primitive forest birds, often though not always found far from water, have broader, flatter beaks often with a slightly hooked tip. Typical of these forest kingfishers are the Kookaburras of Australia and the White-breasted (Smyrna) Kingfisher of Asia.

Clearly, however, to do justice to over 8,000 species and their habitats requires more than just a chapter — several volumes would be needed. So what follows is but a summary, brief in the extreme, but offering some sort of window on the birds of the world and their measureless range of colours, sizes, habits and adaptations — enough to whet the appetite for more.

Those concerned as specialists with the world distribution of animals and plants have divided the globe into regions. For the animals, zoogeographers usually recognise a series based on the studies of two nineteenth-century British zoologists, Philip Lutley Sclater and Alfred Russell Wallace. Their regions (or realms) sometimes cross the boundaries of continents as we know them, and subsequent workers have added to or modified the original concepts, but only in slight degree. The birds, too, cannot be expected to adhere strictly to manmade rules: the existence amongst birds in particular of so many well-established long-range migrations gives a clear indication of this. So the 'typical' birds of one region may be joined by some of those typical of another region during their non-breeding season. The commonly-accepted regions are:

Nearctic	North America
Neotropical	Central and South America
Palaearctic	Europe, the vastness of central
	and northern Asia, Arabia and
	the northern fringe of Africa
Oriental	southern and southeastern Asia
Australasia	Australia, New Zealand and New Guinea
	and associated islands

To this list is often added Antarctica, and some would argue that an Oceanic realm is desirable to cater for the seabirds, although these are only about 285 species among 8,600 odd, and for the various island dwellers.

These have developed as insular species, differing from island to island in some cases, reaching adaptive extremes like the Flightless Cormorant of the Galapagos in others, and in yet other (particularly fascinating) cases, showing a wide range of evolutionary trends leading to a group of related species in just one collection of islands. Of the last, the best-known are the Darwin's Finches of the Galapagos, situated on the Equator west of Ecuador. Darwin's Finches range in size from that of a small warbler to as big as a Hawfinch, and although similarly drab in plumage have evolved beak structures, shapes and feeding habits as diverse as those of warbler, Redpoll, Hawfinch and woodpecker. In Hawaii, the Honeycreepers have radiated similarly over time, and also from a postulated single ancestral stock — perhaps a storm-driven flock of migrants, though no obvious mainland ancestors from which they could have been derived exist today. On both the Galapagos and on Hawaii, these ancestors found a range of habitats unexploited by small birds, and in evolving diversified to fill most available feeding 'niches'. Some, not surprisingly, 'overdid' their specialisation, becoming too committed to a chosen way of life and paying the penalty for this, becoming extinct. Eight of the known 22 Honeycreeper species on Hawaii have gone this way, but the remainder show as much variation as the

Darwin's Finches, but with the addition of species with long, down-curved beaks and brush-tipped tongues suitable for nectar feeding.

There are a number of remarkably cosmopolitan birds; not many, though, and perhaps not what would be expected. The Swallow, a long-range migrant and aerial feeder, is one; the Osprey, also a migrant but a specialist fish-eater, is another. More strange is the breadth of range of the Barn Owl — a relatively stay-at-home bird — and its many subspecies. One recent addition to the list would be the Starling, but most of this bird's spread is the result of foolhardy (in hindsight) introductions of the species by man to give human immigrants in new colonies a feeling of home! Another, in this case unaided, is the Cattle Egret, which has become a global bird in the astonishingly short time of 60 years. Ancestral populations in Africa gave rise to birds storm-driven across the Atlantic to South America, where colonisation was well under way by 1937. The narrow isthmus of Central America was reached in 1947, the Great Lakes and beyond in the late 1950s. From other ancestral stock in south-east Asia, colonists penetrated down the island chain to the south-east reaching the Celebes and Sumatra in 1948, Australia in 1963. The Cattle Egret has already been described as an adaptable bird; further evidence of this lies in its colonisation of the newly-cleared forests of South America. The grassland that succeeded the forest had no native small herons to offer competition in the search for small amphibians and reptiles and large insects, so the Cattle Egret's success was ensured.

Although, because of migration or simple overlap of ranges, adjacent zoogeographic regions may share some species, others are peculiar to one or another. Thus 'our' Wren (the Winter Wren to Americans), *Troglodytes troglodytes*, is common across North America (Nearctic), Europe and Asia (Palaearctic), whereas the Short-billed Marsh Wren occurs in both North (Nearctic) and South (Neotropic) America. These are staggering ranges, the one east-west, the other north-south, for such tiny birds. In contrast, the Zapata Wren never leaves its Zapata swamp home in Cuba, nor does the massive (thrush-sized) Cactus Wren stray far from appropriate desert habitat in the south-western USA and Mexico.

Apart from Antarctica, the zoogeographic regions are so vast that they each encompass a tremendous variety of climates, habitats and features of physical geography. In consequence, each contains a wide range of bird species, though those regions lying principally in the tropics tend to contain more species. As a general rule seemingly observed by most plant and animal groups, tropical regions contain more species (but usually lesser numbers of individuals of each species) than temperate zones, where the species count is less but larger numbers of any given species might often be expected.

129

Many bird families, particularly those of any size, are represented in more than one zoogeographic zone, often by quite different members of the family (except where it is migrants that are involved). Even so, there are some groups of birds either peculiar to a particular zoogeographic region, or so dominant there that they deserve special mention. An excellent example would be the wide range of Nearctic (North American) Parulid and Dendroica 'wood warblers'. These, or many of them, are migrants to South America and have a dual notoriety for their beauty of plumage in spring, and for the problems in identifying them in autumn when the plumages of many species are remarkably similar. Some, such as the Bananaquit, have particularly fascinating names. Other American specialities include the Burrowing Owl, largely terrestrial in its habits and with long athletic legs which fit its environment, and the Sapsuckers, woodpeckers which drill holes and then drink the sap that accumulates in them.

The 'New World' of North and South America holds all the species of two large families — the Tyrant Flycatchers and the Icterids. The Tyrants as a group are probably tropical in origin, and although considered rather primitive have expanded to fill the Americas from Patagonia to Alaska with 365 broad-billed insect-eating species, most sporting some sort of distinctive crest, though few can be so striking as the gold-crowned Great Kiskadee or as exotic as the Northern Royal Flycatcher, with its scarlet and grey inch-long fan spread from ear to ear. Though there are fewer Icterids (94 species), the family includes many birds as familiar to North Americans as Blackbirds are to us, and one group, though in no way related, they call 'Blackbirds'. Perhaps Icterids can best be likened to a wide range of Starlings — most, for example, have the same purposeful walk (rather than hopping) as the Starling, and, on a variety of size scales, the same sort of dagger-like beak. Meadowlarks, the Baltimore Oriole and the Bobolink (another fascinating name) are popular country birds, but the Red-winged Blackbird, ancestrally and even now typically a marshland species, has become a serious pest of cereal crops, the more damaging because of the huge numbers (often millions) in which it descends on the prairies. In the tropics of South America, larger (crow-sized) members of the Icterid family, the Oropendolas and Caciques, are amongst the bird world's master builders. Oropendolas are colonial nesters, choosing an outstandingly tall tree, towering above the canopy, in which to build their pendant nests. They weave grasses into a long sleeve, with the entrance at the top, near the point of suspension from a branch. At the base of this sleeve — 3-6 feet (1-2 m) below — the nest chamber is formed. Oropendolas are often gaudily coloured, and usually noisy. The colony has a complex social structure, with females considerably outnumbering males, which perch at the top of the tree as a flock of sentinels, collectively sharing the duties of guarding the colony and fathering the young.

Two equally colourful families are primarily South American, or Neo-tropical, in origin. The hummingbirds, often called flying jewels, are perhaps the most dazzlingly colourful of all the bird families, with a beautiful iridescence setting them apart from everything except the Old World sunbirds. So attractive and tiny were they that many species in the past have been endangered by collectors seeking skins for costume jewellery, and in Victorian times there is a record of one London dealer importing over 400,000 skins in a single year from the West Indies. Hummingbirds range in size from the Bee Hummingbirds, fractionally over 2 in (5 cm) long and weighing 2 grams (or 14 to the ounce), to the Giant Hummingbird (one of the drabbest in plumage) which is as long as a Song Thrush at 8 in (20 cm) and lives high in the Andes. Of over 300 species, only a dozen or so have penetrated into North America, but in South America they have adapted to a wide range of habitats from the steaming heat of the jungle up to the snow line. Most are nectar or insect feeders, and some have enormously extended tubular beaks, as long or longer than their bodies, to reach nectar at the base of trumpet-shaped flowers. With their renowned flying abilities (they are able to hover, and even fly 'in reverse', more effectively than a Harrier jet fighter) they have high energy demands, and have developed special survival stratagems. These are most needed by northern or high-altitude species, which tend to go into a torpor (a mini-hibernation if you like) overnight, cutting down heartbeat and respiration to minimal levels, reducing energy output, until warmed back to normal life by next day's sunshine.

The tanagers (over 200 species) are mostly thrush-sized or smaller, and like the hummingbirds are primarily sedentary species from tropical South America, although 4 species have developed a migratory route into North America. Their beak structures range from flycatcher-like to finch-like, with many intermediates, and their diet seems to be a catholic mixture of insects, often caught in flight, and various fruits and berries. They range in colour from one end of the rainbow spectrum to the other, sometimes all on the same bird (Paradise Tanager and Blue-crowned Chlorophonia for example), with a pre-dominance of blues that typifies South American birds but which is strangely much less common in birds from other regions.

South America contains some of the richest country avifaunas to be found anywhere in the world, with several lists well in excess of 1,000 species. Naturally there are some oddities, such as the ovenbird family, with its old-fashioned bread-oven-shaped mud nests, and the Hoatzin. The Hoatzin is primitive, feeble in flight and nests beside water. If danger threatens, the young drop from the nest into the water below, emerging when the danger has passed to scramble back up into the trees using a hooked claw — a sort of vestigial thumb — on the wing angle to help them do this.

131

Crossing the South Atlantic Ocean to Africa (the Ethiopian zoogeographic region) we find almost as diverse an avifauna (enriched by many migrants in winter from the Palaearctic) which is almost as colourful as that of South America. The sunbirds (unrelated, but ecological parallels to the hummingbirds) are an example, as are the bee-eaters. Neither family is restricted to Africa, but each is best and most widely developed there, with over half of the species represented. Unlike the Americas, it is difficult to find a bird family of any size

Bee-eaters

which is restricted to Africa, although several (such as the shrikes and hornbills) besides the two already mentioned are to be seen at their best here. The 19 species of Touraco are an exception; most are brightly coloured, pigeon-sized forest birds, renowned for the deep crimson flashes in their wings. This pigment (called turacin) is peculiar to the touracos and is water-soluble: a touraco feather stirred around in a glass of water leaves it stained pink.

South of the Sahara desert, Africa is very rich in birds. The lowland rain-forests, although now much changed by man, stretch in a broad belt across the middle of the Continent and hold many of the more-specialised birds, such as the touracos. The various lakes and swamps of the Nile drainage area and the great Rift Valley, running north-south the length of the Continent, hold a spectacular array of waterbirds and the semi-arid veldt and bushy savannas support immense numbers of small seed-eating birds. One species of the large weaver bird family is probably the most numerous kind of bird in the world, and also the most damaging avian agricultural pest. The Black-faced Dioch, or *Quelea*, occurs in enormous flocks, often millions of birds strong and looking in flight like a plague of locusts, feeding, breeding and roosting gregariously, and ranging over much of south and central Africa. *Quelea* damage various cereal crops, particularly guinea corn, both by eating the grains and in causing 'physical' damage by collapsing the crop under the sheer weight of numbers in the flocks. Cultivated cereals seem not to be preferred food; smaller seeds of various wild grasses form the bulk of the diet. Even in years of severe damage, only 20 per cent of *Quelea* food intake may be of cultivated cereals.

The widespread and vast areas producing wild seed in the rainy seasons are exploited by many animals, but it is only towards the end of dry seasons that food shortage forces *Quelea* flocks into the river valleys and inundation zones favoured for agricultural crops. The 'last straw' comes at the onset of the rains, when any remaining seeds promptly germinate and the *Quelea* flocks face starvation. This provokes a merging of already-large flocks, and causes nomadic migrations in search of areas where earlier rains have replenished seed stocks, both wild and cultivated. On these, the vast and ravenously destructive hordes descend: to such effect that in South Africa damage was devastating in one year despite the poisoning of an estimated 100 million *Quelea* by aerial sprays.

The desert areas, too, have their specialist birds. The sandgrouse are good examples, again well-represented in Africa but with outlying species in southern Europe (where they are scarce) and in southern Asia, where, as in Africa, they may occur in huge flocks. Although they nest out in the desert, they may fly considerable distances each day to waterholes to drink — often tens of miles. Some species supply their young with water in a unique way. At the water hole, an adult, having drunk its fill, will wade into the shallows, allowing the water to soak up into its belly feathers as if into a sponge. It then sets off, flying rapidly as always, back to its nest, where the young wriggle beneath their parent and suck the water from the feathers.

The Oriental region includes the Indian sub-continent, south-east Asia and

133

the vast stretches of China and the neighbouring countries. Much of it is less ornithologically explored than other parts of the globe, but even so, with a habitat range spanning the Himalayas and their foothills, monsoon forests, mangrove swamps, steppes and deserts, the bird fauna is, as expected, very rich. As with Africa, relatively few sizeable bird families are restricted to the region. Of those that are, the leafbirds, brilliantly coloured forest birds, about Song Thrush size, are the most melodious, many being excellent songsters. They are nectar and fruit eaters, and glory in elaborate names as well as plumages, like Fairy Bluebird, Iora, and Golden-fronted Leafbird. The pittas, 23 species of them, are just as colourful but generally rather larger. Like giant but tail-less wrens, the pittas scurry about on the rain-forest floor, keeping to the darkest and densest undergrowth, where sadly their secretive habits allow only fleeting and poor views of their spectacular plumages.

Of the families of wider distribution but best represented in the Oriental region, it is the pheasants and their relatives that most deserve mention. This is the home of the Peacock, and of several Jungle Fowl species, the probable ancestors of our domestic chickens, and sounding just like our birds as their crowing starts the jungle 'dawn chorus'. Most colourful, however, even in this galaxy of colour, are the pheasants. Golden and Silver Pheasants have names indicative of their splendour (though omitting many of the other rich colours they sport) but others, like Reeves, Lady Amherst, and Swinhoe's Pheasants, are just as gloriously spectacular, and for this reason are often to be found in bird collection aviaries all round the world.

Naturally enough, as the climate becomes more severe with rising altitude in the Himalayas, the birds become fewer and more specialised. Several of the laughing thrushes ascend almost to the tree line, and the Alpine Chough well beyond it. Spectacular altitude feats are achieved by Ruppell's Griffon Vulture, recorded at over 33,000 feet (10,000 m) and by the Bar-headed Goose, commonly kept in waterfowl collections, which breeds north of the mountains and migrates south, routinely it seems flying at great heights, though perhaps not often at the altitude of a flock seen by climbers on Annapurna at about 28,000 feet (8,500 m), an astonishing performance taking account of the lack of oxygen in such circumstances.

Thus we come to the Australasian region, renowned for its range of marsupials, or pouched primitive mammals, whose presence indicates the length of time the region has been isolated. Although such isolation is less complete for birds than for terrestrial mammals, Australasia does have a number of groups of birds found nowhere else. Amongst these are the large and flightless Emu of the open plains and bush, and the three Cassowary species, which live deep in forests. These can all run at speeds up to 30 mph (48 kph) and, surprisingly, can swim well. The Cassowaries are aggressive, even to man, attacking feet-first with slashing kicks that have killed numbers of local natives. Smaller, and more restricted in distribution, are the three chicken-sized Kiwis of New Zealand, which are noteworthy not just as the international symbol of their homeland but because they are one of the few birds to possess, and use in their nocturnal worm-hunting forays, an acute sense of smell (the nostrils are situated, unusually, at the tip of the beak) and because the female lays probably the largest egg, for its size, of any bird. The egg is about 5 in (12.5 cm) long, and weighs about 1 lb (0.5 kg) — of the order of one quarter of the female's body weight. After the effort of laying it, the unfortunate bird must then incubate it for about 90 days — another feat of endurance! Kiwis, too, are flightless swampy forest dwellers, anatomically very different from the other flightless species living today, and perhaps related only to the gigantic Moas that existed in New Zealand until hunted to extinction by the Maoris some 700 years ago.

Other well-known Australasian specialities include the Lyrebirds, two chicken-sized forest species whose males sport a tail composed of two long curled feathers like the arms of a lyre, or harp, and many equally long gossamer-fine plumes, which are held forward over the head during the complex courtship display dance. This takes place on a well-trodden, regularly used arena, and here the Lyrebird exercises to the full its extraordinary talents as a mimic. Besides some song and calls of its own, the displaying Lyrebird incorporates many other forest bird songs and calls (with confusing accuracy) as well as man-made artefacts (like saw cutting, wolf whistles, axe blows and car horns) and rural sounds like bleating sheep or barking dogs!

The Lyrebirds are drably coloured, but another Australasian group, the tiny Wren-Warblers (about the size of a Long-tailed Tit), are quite the opposite. There are about 80 species, small-bodied but with a long, jauntily cocked tail, the males sharing between them most of the colours of the rainbow. They tend to live in groups, with one dominant male in full plumage, a few secondary males (whose plumage more resembles the drabber camouflage colours of the female) and several females. Wren-warblers are not fast flyers, and should the dominant male, so conspicuous in plumage, be caught by a bird of prey the next male in the order of succession promptly moults into full and glorious plumage and assumes leadership of the troupe.

The largest of the families peculiar to this region is the honeyeaters. Of the 160 species, most are thrush-sized or smaller. Although their plumages vary from the gaudy to the drab, their songs are usually well-developed and pleasing to the human ear. All have long, slender, down-curved beaks and a long, protrusible tongue. This has a brush-like tip to collect nectar, and the sides of the tongue can be rolled in, like a drinking straw, to convey the collected nectar to the gut.

With so many species, there are honeyeaters everywhere there are nectar-producing plants, shrubs or trees.

Although this chapter has seen a galaxy of colours, surely the Birds of Paradise must be the most colourful and ornate family in the entire world of birds. They live in the forests of Van Wa Tu (New Guinea) and its adjacent islands and have long been threatened because of their beauty — first by the natives of the islands, and later by the so-called 'civilised world', in each case seeking spectacular ornamentation. There are 40 living species, several named after royalty or the nobility (Queen Victoria's Riflebird, Count Raggi's, Prince Rudolph's and Princess Stephanie's Birds of Paradise, for example). They range in size from the 6-in (15-cm) King to the 42-in (105-cm) Ribbon-tailed Bird of Paradise, which is the largest of the Passerines, or true perching birds. Spectacular colours are matched by filamentous plumes, exposed only during display as a shimmering haze of colour, and often the effects are enhanced by strange postures and song. The Blue Bird of Paradise, from high in the mountains, hangs upside down beneath a gauzy curtain of blue plumes, producing the most astonishing cascade of song at the same time. So metallic and alien-sounding is the song that it is difficult to attribute it to a bird, but its very strangeness adds another dimension to the beauty of these magnificent birds.

Any attempt to produce a gazetteer of good birdwatching localities within these zoogeographic regions is fraught with many difficulties, not least the number that would need listing. However there are some general points that are worth making. Wilderness areas such as Lake Algonquin (famous for Great Northern Divers) in Canada or the Namib Desert in south Africa are often sparsely populated, though with fascinating or spectacular species, and much the same can be said of most forest areas. Farmland (such as much of central Ethiopia), grassland and bush-veldt or scrub can often hold large numbers of birds, but their precise location is governed by the presence of good seed food supplies. A quick mental 'round-the-world-trip' of famous birdwatching areas is revealing. Starting in North America, the Everglades of Florida come to mind; in South America perhaps the Galapagos Islands and the marshes of Guayaquil. In Africa, Lake Nakuru and Lake Naivasha, in Kenya, are noteworthy, and in the Oriental region Bharatpur and the Rhan of Kutch in India. It is more difficult to be selective in Australasia, but the island avifaunas come to mind, as does the wetland around Humpty Doo in North Australia. The point of most interest in this list may be that so many of these famous sites (and add to them the European list) are wetlands. Not only do the wetland areas have their own range of spectacular, often dramatic, birds (such as the millions of Lesser Flamingos on Lake Nakuru) but they seem to attract a broad range of other species. Even most desert birds, such as sandgrouse, have an essential need for water, and this highlights the reason for such places as being excellent starting places to begin an exploration of the birds of a new country.

Further Reading

Austin, O.L. and Singer, A., *Birds of the World*, Hamlyn 1961

Brown, L., *British Birds of Prey*, Collins 1976

Campbell, B. and Ferguson-Lees, I.J., *A Field Guide to Birds Nests*, Constable 1972

Coombs, C.J.F., *The Crows*, Batsford 1978

Cramp, S. and Simmons, K.E.L., *Handbook of the Birds of Europe, the Middle East and North Africa*, Vols. I and II, Oxford University Press, I 1977, II 1980

Cramp, S., Bourne, W.R.P. and Saunders, D., *The Seabirds of Britain and Ireland*, Collins 1974

Durman, R. (ed), *Bird Observatories in Britain and Ireland*, Poyser 1976

Fisher, J. and Flegg, J., *Watching Birds*, Poyser 1974

Fisher, J. and Lockley, R.M., *Seabirds*, Collins 1954

Fleure, H.J., *A Natural History of Man in Britain*, Collins 1951

Freethy, R., *How Birds Work*, Blandford Press 1982

Fuller, R.J., *Bird Habitats in Britain*, Poyser 1982

Gooders, J., *Where To Watch Birds in Britain and Europe*, André Deutsch 1970

Hale, W.G., *Waders*, Collins 1980

Harrison, J.G. and Grant, P., *The Thames Transformed*, André Deutsch 1976

Lack, D., *Ecological Adaptations for Breeding in Birds*, Methuen 1968

Lack, D., *Ecological Isolation in Birds*, Blackwell 1971

Manley, G., *Climate and the British Scene*, Collins 1952

Mead, C.J., *Bird Ringing*, British Trust for Ornithology 1974

Murton, R.K., *Man and Birds*, Collins 1971

Newton, I., *Finches*, Collins 1972

Newton, I., *Population Ecology of Raptors*, Poyser 1979

Ogilvie, M.A., *Wild Ducks of Britain and Europe*, Poyser 1975

Ogilvie, M.A., *Wild Geese*, Poyser 1978

Parslow, J.L.F., *Breeding Birds in Britain and Ireland*, Poyser 1973

Perrins, C.M., *British Tits*, Collins 1955

Prater, A.J., *Estuary Birds in Britain and Ireland*, Poyser 1981

Sharrock, J.T.R. (ed), *The Atlas of Breeding Birds in Britain and Ireland*, Poyser 1976

Sharrock, J.T.R. and E.M., *Rare Birds in Britain and Ireland*, Poyser 1976

Simms, E., *Woodland Birds*, Collins 1971

Simms, E., *British Thrushes*, Collins 1978

Snow, D.W. (ed), *The Status of Birds in Britain and Ireland*, Blackwell 1971

Stamp, L.D., *Britain's Structure and Scenery*, Collins 1946

Stamp, L.D., *Man and the Land*, Collins 1955

Voons, K.H., *Atlas of European Birds*, Nelson 1960

Whitlock, R., *A Short History of Farming in Britain*, Baker 1965

Wright, E.N., Feare, G.C.J. and Isaacson, A.J., (eds), *Understanding Agricultural Bird Problems*, British Crop Protection Council 1980

Yapp, W.B., *Birds and Woods*, Oxford University Press 1962

Appendix

Birdwatching can be a completely solo pursuit, if you so wish, whether your intention is simply to look at birds and enjoy them against their natural background environment or whether you wish to become involved in a more intensive study of a particular species or habitat. Alternatively, it can be a co-operative enterprise: it would be difficult to deny the social enjoyment that comes from birdwatching in a group, and much of our knowledge of the lives of our birds is derived from the organised co-operative studies of groups of amateurs.

Great Britain
Groups of one or two may be ideal if you want really good views of the birds, but properly organised group outings can be immensely helpful to the beginner, not just by providing expert guidance to bird identification, but also by introducing you to the best local birdwatching spots. So, if you are starting out as a birdwatcher, first find your local club, group or society. These are now very numerous (far too numerous to list) and most fair-sized centres of population will have one. The local public library is the place to ask for details. Most counties will have a society which will publish an annual report of the birds seen in its area: very useful background reading for the newcomer and old hand alike.

Clubs and societies like these often run a series of indoor meetings, with a wide variety of films and speakers, through the winter months, and right through the year field excursions to places of ornithological interest, sometimes within the county, sometimes a day's coach trip away, and (increasingly)

Bird observatories in Britain and Ireland. The major observatories are represented on the Bird Observatories Council, and each provides (at various standards but usually hostel-style) accommodation for birdwatchers wishing to stay overnight. Details of the observatories, and the addresses of their Booking Secretaries, can be obtained by sending a stamped self-addressed envelope to: The Ringing Office, British Trust for Ornithology, Beech Grove, Tring, Hertfordshire.

Ibis) publishes *The Auk.* In America, *Bird Banding* specialises in ringing studies, as does the BTO *Ringing and Migration* in Britain. On a more popular level, the *National Audubon Society* (which broadly resembles the RSPB) produces the lavishly illustrated *Audubon* magazine.

Africa

Africa is not rich in societies, but in the Republic of South Africa the *Ornithological Society* publishes *The Ostrich.*

Australasia

Australia has the *Australian Ornithological Union,* journal *Emu,* and New Zealand an *Ornithological Society* publishing *Notornis.*

Index

Figures in italics refer to page numbers of illustrations.